KINGDOM AUTHORITY

KINGDOM AUTHORITY

Understanding the Bible through the Lens of Authority
as a Child of Light in the Kingdom of Darkness

T. L. BENNINGFIELD

XULON PRESS

Xulon Press
2301 Lucien Way #415
Maitland, FL 32751
407.339.4217
www.xulonpress.com

© 2022 by T. L. Benningfield

All rights reserved solely by the author. The author guarantees all contents are original and do not infringe upon the legal rights of any other person or work. No part of this book may be reproduced in any form without the permission of the author.

Due to the changing nature of the Internet, if there are any web addresses, links, or URLs included in this manuscript, these may have been altered and may no longer be accessible. The views and opinions shared in this book belong solely to the author and do not necessarily reflect those of the publisher. The publisher therefore disclaims responsibility for the views or opinions expressed within the work.

Unless otherwise indicated, Scripture quotations taken from the New American Standard Bible (NASB). Copyright © 1960, 1962, 1963, 1968, 1971, 1972, 1973, 1975, 1977, 1995 by The Lockman Foundation. Used by permission. All rights reserved.

Paperback ISBN-13: 978-1-66286-476-6
Ebook ISBN-13: 978-1-66286-477-3

**To my wife Linda
and
My amazing children Ryan and Emma
Who have all put up with my weirdness for so many years.**

And to my Lord and Savior Jesus, the Christ

Table of Contents

1. LAYING THE FOUNDATION. 1
   Spiritual Experiences. 4
2. WHAT IS AUTHORITY 9
   Types of Authority: 10
   Four Estates of Authority:. 11
   Stages of Authority Illustrated .12
3. AUTHORITY IN CREATION:. 13
   Thousand Years 18
   Patience of God 19
   Adam 19
   Two Accounts. 20
   mDNA. 20
4. AUTHORITY TO IMPART AUTHORITY: 23
   Jesus is God 24
5. AUTHORITY TO IMPART BOUNDARIES: 27
6. AUTHORITY USURPED: 35
   Battlefield of the Mind:. 38
7. AUTHORITY TO IMPART JUDGMENT: 41
   Theological rabbit trial 44
   Back to the Authority to impart judgment. 47
   Satan's Plan to Usurp Authority 48
8. THE AUTHORITY OF JESUS 51
9. THE SPIRITUAL REALM. 57
   Angels and Fallen angels. 57
   Transitioning Authority 63
   How I came to know Jesus 63
   Demons 67

- Seed of the Woman: 69
- Book of Enoch 72
- The Flood 76
- Future Fulfillment:................................84
10. AUTHORITY OF FOLLOWERS OF JESUS....................87
- Two Kingdoms 87
- The Church 93
- Holy Spirit......................................100
- Covering for sin 103
- What happened when Jesus died 105
- A Perspective on Paradise........................107
- Spiritual Gifts 112
- Triune nature of prayer 117
- Study of the Word of God -The Path 121
- Learning to listen...............................125
- Meditating on the Word...........................129
- The Question, the Believer, and the Church 134
- Things to Come 143

Bibliography 151

Chapter 1

LAYING THE FOUNDATION:

I have wanted to write this book for many years, but I kept getting distracted by other things that were not necessarily more important but seemed to take precedent at the time.

My main goal in writing this work is to develop a framework. Like building a computer, you must have the frame before making any sense of the rest of the pieces. The goal is to provide this framework to help you understand the Bible better.

When teaching, I often use the illustration of putting together a puzzle. We first discover and define the edges, and from here, we can begin to understand this big picture. Once we set our edges, it is easier to start filling in the pieces in a way that makes sense. Likewise, once we develop a framework, it is much easier to see how the pieces of the Bible fit together. Another analogy I use comes from my tool chest in my garage. It is easy to make sense of the whole by having a place for everything and everything in its place. Developing this framework makes it much easier for us to make sense of how the Bible fits together as we read and study. We can understand why God dealt with Israel and their neighbors in the various ways He did. Yeah, I know too many metaphors. The point is that we must approach the Bible from different directions to understand it better.

As a Christian, pastor, and evangelist, I have gotten questions over the years, such as, "If God is loving, then why did He tell Israel to kill all those people when they took over a town?" or "If there is a God, then why do bad things happen?" As you continue reading, everything will start to make sense to you. I have always said that I love the question of why. This very word drives us to find answers in any pursuit. It is never a wrong question unless the ears and minds are too closed to receive the response. With that in mind, I pray your ears and mind are open to considering what I have written and that you will have some incredible moments of discovery moving forward.

The main inspiration for this work came from a few times that we went to church when I was a child. We were not a "church-going" family. I do believe that if someone asked my family members when we were growing up if they were Christians, they would have said yes. They would say they believed, but I do not remember any evidence of this belief in our lives. The only time I remember hearing the name of God during that time was when someone would swear. I have no early memories of Christmas or Easter being about Jesus at all. I remember the focal point of those holidays as Santa and the Bunny.

When I was around six or seven years old, my mother sent me to a "Vacation Bible School" type Christmas program in the winter over the holiday season. I remember singing the little drummer boy with the kids up on stage as a performance. At some point during the overall program, they had all of the kids in the program get on their knees at the platform's edge and pray to receive Jesus into our hearts as Lord and Savior. As part of this group, I did as they requested, but I was not "saved" at that time. I had no fundamental understanding of what they were asking for, and I was only complying with the request.

Over the years, there were a few occasions when my mother received an invitation from a friend who invited us to visit their church, and we would go. I believe that only happened twice. The Sunday morning would arrive, and my mother, stepfather, and I would go to the service. My mother would sit strategically in the middle between my stepfather and me so that she could keep us awake. She would continually send her elbows to either side because she would find us dozing off. Yet, from that experience, I have always remembered the pastor's statements during one of those services. I remember hearing that I would go to hell if I did not receive Jesus as my Lord and Savior. I did not overthink it at the time, but later, the statement struck me as odd and somewhat selfish. "God" will send me to hell just for not accepting his Son, Jesus? Wow. Is that a God I would genuinely want to get to know?

I had completely misunderstood the message the preacher was trying to convey. To be honest, I am not sure if I misunderstood the message because of how he presented it or how I received it. For clarity right now, I want you to know this truth. A person goes to hell for one reason and one reason only, because of sin. It is only our sin that separates us from God. Not because of Jesus. Our sin and only our sin separate us from the relationship we are created to have with God. Jesus is not "why" we go to hell; He is the only solution we have to save us from hell.

Jesus came to rescue us from going to hell by paying the debt for sin that you and I owe. I know some may tune out at this point, but I would invite you to continue reading in an effort to understand why I would make such a statement. For example, we are taught in Romans 3:23, "For ALL have sinned and fall short of the glory of God."[1] You and I are separate from God because of sin. If I have ever told a lie, then I am a liar. Lying is a sin. Even that sin would separate me from God. God is completely justified in His judgment concerning me because of that sin. The Way of the Master series by Ray Comfort and Kirk Cameron shares this truth in a simple format. I would encourage you to discover their videos on Youtube. It is worth checking out. I have spent time telling people about Jesus in the streets, and I found I like to keep it simple. As you would see in the video series, they do too.

---

[1] New American Standard Bible: 1995 Update (La Habra, CA: The Lockman Foundation, 1995), All References

Growing up, I would have replied yes if someone had asked me if I believed in Jesus. If they had asked if I thought that Jesus died on the cross for my sins and was risen to life on the third day, I would have replied yes. I did not know much, but I had no trouble believing this. Yet, I was not "saved." It is much the same as believing that a particular person is our president, but you did not vote for them. You know they are the president. You believe this without any doubt, but you never cast your vote for that person.

When I came to know Jesus as Lord was the night when I cast my vote for Him, it was years later, on a night I was cognitive enough to recognize that my life was a mess, that it was in chaos, I finally, as it is often said, "gave my life to Jesus."

My wife and I served as missionaries for six years with an organization called Village Missions. They asked me to write up my story, or "testimony," for one of the publications. A testimony is essentially my personal account of how I came to know Jesus. I titled it "From Chaos to Christ." The night I finally came to know Jesus as my Lord and savior, I felt my life was in chaos. In brief, I remembered what they said to do as that young boy at the Christmas program so many years before. I called out to Jesus for help. He answered me and gave me a vision in two parts. When I came out of that vision, my life was forever changed. I had this experience on March 17th, 1984. I will tell you more about this later, too.

Spiritual Experiences

When it comes to having spiritual experiences, I have found that some people seem to have them more than others. I will share some of my experiences with you throughout this book. I believe that some people are wired a little closer to the edge of spiritual things than others. I do not know why this is true, but I have come to see and believe it.

LAYING THE FOUNDATION:

Even before I believed in Jesus, I had spiritual experiences. More so after. On the other side of this "spiritual experience" spectrum, I know people who have absolutely no recognition of spiritual things whatsoever. Their whole experience is what they can feel, see, taste, touch, and hear. These people seem void of any sense of spiritual discernment. I am not faulting them or considering them less than, for lack of a better term, it is how just they are wired, and that is okay. I am sure they are gifted in many other areas. One of the goals I would hope to accomplish by writing this book would be to move them to considering the truth of the spiritual realm.

I initially chose the title for this book: "The Heart of the Gospel." I was working on an idea for a master's thesis in the Seminary. This was back in the mid-nineties. The question we were to answer for our thesis was what we believed is the main topic of the Bible. When I read the Bible, I see that the primary overall theme is one of authority. The authority of God stands out above everything else. From Genesis to Revelation, I see the main message that God is Sovereign, and He alone has ultimate authority. There is none above Him. His authority runs through scriptures from the beginning to the end.

Out of necessity, as we talk about God's sovereign authority, we will also talk about the different aspects of the spiritual realm, the fall of man to sin, the consequence of separation from God, and many other areas to lay a foundation of understanding.

As I grew and understood more about the Bible and this person, Jesus, one of the truths I realized was that misconception I had so many years ago. God was not sending me or anyone else to hell because we did not accept his son, as I mentioned earlier. The only reason we were bound for hell was because of our sin. My sin separated me from God. Jesus came on a rescue mission to save me from that inevitable outcome by paying the debt I owed for my sin. Romans 6:23 reads, "For the wages of sin is death, but the free gift of God is eternal life in Christ Jesus our Lord." If sin separated me from God, then sin has to be removed for me to experience the relationship I was created to have with God.

In truth, there was nothing I could do to remove my sin. The wages or consequence of my sin was this separation from God and spiritual death. In our context, what does death mean? As an introduction to this topic, we should know that two types of death exist. One is physical death, and one is spiritual death. Physical death is the cessation of life in the physical body and is self-explanatory. Spiritual death means eternal separation from God. It also means everlasting punishment for the sin I have committed. It can also mean everlasting life for those who receive the forgiveness offered through the sacrifice of Jesus on their behalf.

The answer to my eternal predicament could not come from me. The only payment for sin is death. It is not a "work vs. sin" balance scale. I could perform millions of good works, and it would never remove a single sin that I have committed. The only option I had was to pay for my sin. Changing that outcome would require the death I owe for sin to come from somewhere else. Someone else would have to pay my debt for me. The problem is every other human being has their own sin debt to pay. Since they have their own debt, they could not pay mine. Having an obligation of their own, they were not qualified to pay for my sin. For someone else to pay my sin debt, they would have to have no debt of their own to pay. Having no debt of their own to pay would free them up to pay my debt. That is where Jesus comes in.

God took it upon Himself to provide the payment for our sin. This payment can free us from our debt and allow us to experience reconciliation in our relationship with Him. <u>He</u> provided the way. We just needed to understand it, trust it, and receive it. God is a God of love, mercy, grace, and reconciliation. His desire to be reconciled with every one of us is motivated by His unyielding love for us. AND He can carry out His plan for our salvation, that is, "to save us" by His <u>authority.</u> This authority, KINGDOM AUTHORITY, is at the heart of the Gospel.

LAYING THE FOUNDATION:

It is essential to understand that while God is loving, He is also a just, holy, and righteous God. God will pour out His judgment for sin at the appointed time. The payment of death that is due because of sin must be paid. The choice is simple; we pay the debt for our sin ourselves or accept God's payment on our behalf. The death we own is the death that Jesus paid. Jesus was the only one eligible to pay our debt. Why you might ask, is it because He was sinless? The answer is yes. Jesus lived here and walked this earth as a man and never once committed sin. Since He had no sin to pay for Himself, He is eligible to pay for the sins of others. Others like you and me. Yet, He was not a man separated from God. Jesus is God. We will talk more about this as we move on. In His humanity, he was eligible to pay for our sin. Yet, as God, He was not under the authority of the enemy of God, who has taken possession of this world.

It is essential to understand that as a man sinned, in the beginning, cutting off our relationship with God, it has to be a man to restore this relationship. Romans 5:12 reads, "Therefore, just as through one man sin entered into the world, and death through sin, and so death spread to all men because all sinned."[2] Sin removed us from the relationship we were supposed to have with God. We were under His authority and walking with God. Sin broke this relationship and placed us under the authority of Satan. We were held under this authority in bondage because of sin. Jesus, being God, was not under this authority.

So to recap, for humankind to be free from the consequence of sin, there must be an alternative payment for sin. Jesus is that payment. We must receive that payment to our account. Our debt has been satisfied, for our relationship with God is restored. It had to be someone who had no sin of their own to pay. Jesus is one hundred percent a man. As such, He was qualified to redeem fallen humanity. Likewise, He is also one hundred percent God. As such, He was not under the authority of Satan. More on this later.

---

[2] Ibid. Romans 5:12

As I mentioned, when I was in seminary back in the mid-nineties, we were asked to come up with what we believed the theme of the Bible was. Many came up with answers like love, grace, and redemption. When I first shared my answer to the question, it raised a few eyebrows, and I got more than a few puzzled looks. Yet, I see the authority of God through every aspect of the Bible, and it is this authority that will bring the very promises of God to fruition. This authority of God guarantees we can trust in the promises of God as believers in the Lord Jesus, our Christ. Proof of this authority is not only demonstrated but proven through scriptures.

In the following pages, I want to take a journey with you to understand authority and how it impacts the Word of God and the overall message conveyed in the Bible. The goal is to unpack some of the pieces of the Bible puzzle in such a way that it provides you with some "Ah-ha" moments. My hope is to increase the knowledge, faith, and perspective of all who read.

I am not seeking to provide a complete comprehensive account of authority in this book. Likewise, my goal is to keep this easy to read and understand. I only want to give enough to help you understand the reality of and have confidence in the plan of God and the victory of those who have placed their faith in the Lord Jesus.

I seek to help you, the reader, understand that there is a God, and He has authority. While this world may seem chaotic and upside down, there are real reasons for this, but ultimately God will bring his purposeful end to his predetermined conclusion

Chapter 2

WHAT IS AUTHORITY:

When we talk about authority, it is also necessary to talk about power. These two are not the same. We should understand that there is a difference between power and authority. For many, it is hard to understand the distinction. I want to give you a rather simplistic definition I came up with that I believe is helpful for our discussion, "Power is the ability to subject, authority is the permission to do so." Because a person or group has the power to do something does not mean they have the authority to do it. For example, a mob may have the ability or power to take control of an area of a city, but this does not mean they have the authority to do so. Laws, for example, have authority, but if they are void of enforcement, they have no power.

I wanted to start here for a particular reason. I want you to know and understand that if you are a follower of Jesus, while the enemies of God appear to have an enormous amount of power, they do not have authority over us. We will talk more about this later. For now, know at the outset that victory is certain.

With authority, there are different levels of power that people display. In America, the Commander in Chief is the president of the United States. The president has been granted power. Yet, by design, he is supposed to be under the authority of the American people.

From their citizenship, he derives his authority, which places him in a position of power. From this position of power, he is to act on behalf of the American people. As long as he retains this authority granted by the people, he can maintain a position of power. We find an easy and accurate illustration of the distinction between authority and power through government. When it comes to developing an understanding of the heart of the gospel, we need to see it from a two-kingdom perspective. However, another topic we are building to. We will talk about these two kingdoms shortly.

Types of Authority:

Different types of authority are taught in the world and in the Bible. The first of which is the absolute authority of God. This type of authority is called absolutism. Absolutism is often used to describe a secular perspective of monarchy rule. A monarchy is not restrained in power by a constitution. At one point in history, a king may have said off with his head, which was carried out according to his will with no recourse. A constitution can create a division of power. England maintains a Monarchy, though today, the monarchy has been subjugated to parliamentary rule. The parliament has supreme legal authority. In this case, it has become a constitutional monarchy. In the case of God, God has not received authority from any other party. It is His alone. His authority is of Himself. As such, it is absolute.

The second type of authority is the God can impart authority to others. We see this in the example of Adam and Eve. God gave them authority over the world He created for them. They have authority over everything that He has given them, yet they are still under the authority of God. In Genesis 1:28, God said, "God blessed them; and God said to them, "Be fruitful and multiply, and fill the earth, and subdue it; and rule over the fish of the sea and over the birds of the sky and over every living thing that moves on the earth."[3] You can see that God imparted authority to this first family over all that God had created in this world.

The third is a type of usurped authority. It is called Usurpation, and it is, by definition, the illegal encroachment or assumption of the use of authority, power, or property properly belonging to another. For our purpose. Authority can be seized even legally by those who do not have the best interests of God or this world He created in mind. They have their interests in mind, not the welfare of those they oversee. Satan used deception and caused Adam and Eve to sin and sever their relationship with God. This severance caused a change of authority. All of the authority that God gave them passed over to Satan. He became the one in authority over the world and everything in it. The authority that God gave them in Genesis 1:28 passed over to Satan, and they, in turn, became subject to the authority of Satan as part of this world. The world at that time was cast into spiritual darkness.

We see this occur many times in scripture from a perspective of world events. Throughout scripture, Israel would turn away from God, and an occupying force would come in and lay hold of them, placing them into bondage, in servitude. They took authority over Israel.

Four Estates of Authority:

The idea of an estate is the title and transference of ownership. In this case, we delineate ownership by the aspect of authority.

The first estate of authority identifies God in authority over mankind and mankind in authority over the earth. The second estate of authority, resulting from the fall, places Satan in the line of authority. God in authority over Satan, Satan in authority over mankind and the world. The third estate of authority is divided. There is a distinction between those who come to know Jesus and those who do not. The

---

[3] Ibid. Genesis 1:28

ones who come to receive Jesus and have their sin account cleansed are taken out from under Satan's authority. They have been brought under the authority of Jesus. This is important to understand. It is here that our victory over the adversary begins. Those who do not come to know Jesus remain in the second estate, under the authority of Satan. The fourth estate will be when the Son turns all things back over to the Father. 1 Corinthians 15:24 reads, "then *comes* the end, when He hands over the kingdom to *our* God and Father when He has abolished all rule and all authority and power."[4]

Stages of Authority Illustrated

    ORIGINAL CREATION:
        1st estate: God -> Man -> World

    FALL OF MAN:
        2nd estate: God -> Satan -> Man -> World

    REDEMPTION THROUGH JESUS:
        3rd estate: a. Unsaved: God -> Satan -> Man -> World
        b. Saved: Jesus -> Those Redeemed

    RESTORATION TO COME:
        4th estate: God -> Man -> New World

---

[4] Ibid 1 Cor 15:21

Chapter 3

AUTHORITY IN CREATION:

I have heard it said many times over the years, and rightly so that God did not need to ask for anyone's permission to create. We only need to read the opening of Genesis to get this, "In the beginning, God." He did not seek consent. He merely acted of his own volition to accomplish everything He desired to achieve. It was in his authority to do so. God has both absolute authority and absolute power to create. He decides according to the course of his own will and uses his own power to bring his creation into existence.

This is important for us to understand. From the very first line of scripture, we see that God is the one who is in charge. He is the one who has complete authority to set a plan into motion. He is also the only one with the power to carry it out.

Often, I get questions from people asking, "If there is a God, then why...?" I am a Marvel movie fan. Superhero movies are generally good action entertainment. I love the Marvel movie "Infinity War." In this movie, there is a scene where Dr. Strange sat for an extended period of time, evaluating fourteen million possibilities and outcomes. In the end, he gave the villain, Thanos; an item called the Time Stone because that was the only option for a victorious result. You could literally hear the audience gasp wondering, what are you doing? Yet, it would not be until the next Avengers film, "End Game" that we clearly understood the reason for this.

Something we must understand about God is that He is eternal. There are over seventy verses that talk about the eternal nature of God. For example, Psalm 48:14, "Our God forever and ever."

God is eternal, and as such, He exists outside of time. Time is part of God's framework for us to exist within. He knows the beginning and the end of all things. He lives outside of time and can see the entire timeline all of the time. Isaiah 46:10 reads, "Declaring the end from the beginning, and from ancient times things which have not been done, Saying, 'My purpose will be established, And I will accomplish all My good pleasure."

Being eternal, God exists outside of what we commonly call the timeline. Time was created for the rest of creation to exist within. Time provides boundaries, a beginning, and an end. I really appreciate Dr. Kent Hovind. Dr. Hovind teaches creation science education. He has a way of making the difficult simple to understand. One of the truths he teaches is that God created a trinity of trinities. He created three; time, space, and matter. Time exists as three, past, present, and future. Space likewise exists as height, width, and depth. Matter exists as solid, liquid, and gas. It is a trinity of trinities.

God had to have a place to put the things He would create. He had to have a timeline in which to place them, and He had to create something from which He would create everything. God created this framework, "exnihilo," out of nothing. It was only then that He created inside this framework He had designed.

I used to love building Personal Computers. I have built a few dozen computers over the years. When I started making a computer, the first part I needed was the case. I had to have someplace to put all of the other components required for a successful working computer. So, when I heard Dr. Hovind's explanation of the trinity of trinities, it made sense to me. I was able to understand the perspective. I had understood this concept from biblical study over the years. I just liked how concise and easy the "trinity of trinities" approach was to comprehend.

On this topic of discussion, allow me to take a rabbit trail for a moment on creation. While in one of my Seminary classes, a professor made the statement to our class that it did not matter whether the creation account was accurate or not. He stated it did not even matter whether there was a literal Adam and Eve or not. He told us he leaned away from this idea because of the order of the account of creation. He stated that the Genesis account teaches that light was created on day one, yet the planets were not created until day four. For all his wisdom, my professor did not understand what was being taught in scripture. What we are taught on day one is that God created time. The planets were created on day four to govern the time that God created on day one. When I shared this with him, he asked how I could I say that. I said I didn't. The Bible does. In Genesis 1:18, we are taught,

> "God made the two great lights, the greater light to **govern** the day, and the lesser light to **govern** the night; *He made* the stars also. [17] God placed them in the expanse of the heavens to give light on the earth, [18] and to **govern the day and the night**, and to separate the light from the darkness; and God saw that it was good

So again, time was created on the first day. According to in Genesis 1:3-5,

> "Then God said, "Let there be light"; and there was light. [4] God saw that the light was good, and God separated the light from the darkness. [5] God called the light day, and the darkness He called night. And there was evening, and there was morning, one day.

So on day one, time was established. It was the cycle of darkness and light. The planets were created on day four to govern the time that was created on day one. To be fair, this has confused many over the years, but when we let scripture interpret scripture, it all comes together in a way that casts light (pun intended) and brings understanding.

Sometimes I hear people talk about the age of a day. That is, how long was each day of creation? I have heard some say that it could have been millions of years. But this is just not the case at all. We already know that God created time on the first day. The day was a fixed period of duration " that the planets were created to govern, Genesis 1:5 "God called the light day, and the darkness He called night. And there was evening, and there was morning, one day. The planets managed the time that already existed since day one. Apart from a couple of miracles, there is no evidence of any change in the length of the day at any time since the first mention of the day was used. The only change that occurred was moving from the lunar to the Gregorian calendar.

Certainly, in their wisdom, men have developed different theories to try and accommodate the secular idea of an old earth or even include versions of evolution. This is not necessary. Men have come up with ideas like the gap and day-age theories. But once again, we must allow scripture to speak for itself.

I will give a few things to consider. We need to understand that everything God created He created with the presence of age. He made full-grown animals, fruit-bearing trees, and adult or at least not infant humans. This creation includes rocks and hills. We also need to understand the role of catastrophic events in determining age, seemingly evidenced in carbon dating. Did you know iron tools have been discovered in coal beds that are supposed to predate mankind? An iron wheel impression was recently discovered in Russia in a layer determined to be three hundred million years old.

What impact would a catastrophic event make on such a "man-made" tool? Consider the impact of such a catastrophic event as occurred in the days of Noah. In Genesis 7:11-12, we read,

> *"In the six hundredth year of Noah's life, in the second month, on the seventeenth day of the month, on the same day all the fountains of the great deep burst open, and the floodgates of the sky were opened. The rain fell upon the earth for forty days and forty nights."*

What would be the effect of the ground splitting open and water coming forth? How catastrophic for the planet just having a massive wall of water crashing over everything, the incredible destruction, let alone moving soil, potentially creating continents, and burying cities while submerging everything. The layers of resulting sediment even hundreds of feet deep in areas. How extreme were the earth's layout and composition changed with the earth breaking open and spewing forth water?

We human beings like to put forth theories as if they are facts. I see articles all the time discussing a cave drawings and making a complete prehistoric culture. Maybe it was teenagers of ages past hanging out, getting drunk in the cave, and drawing on the wall. We come along and interpret their drawing as a new type of human species. We make conjectures all the time. For example, what have you been taught about the core of the earth? Yet, it is all theory. No one, literally, no one, has even penetrated the crust of the earth. It is speculation. It is a hypothesis, to be sure, but wholly unproven. I know this is hard for people to accept because you have been raised with this idea like I was. I am not saying it is inaccurate. Earth certainly could have a massive molten core. I am saying that it is not a proven theory. Yet, we still hear theories presented as facts about planets far off in the Galaxies when it is all just theory.

When it comes to the days of creation, I want to allow scripture to take the lead. It is important to stand on what the Word of God has to say, and then we can make inferences based on that. What we cannot do is present our inferences as fact. We have to state that based on what is written, we speculate, assume, and believe that this other thing may indeed be true. We are provided no evidence that a change in the day's length has occurred.

Thousand Years

Some people have said a day to the Lord is a thousand years based on 2 Peter 3:8. This was not a literal meaning of the age of a day, today, or at the time of creation. It speaks to the timelessness of God. However, a traveling companion of Paul, whom you are probably familiar with, went by the name of Barnabas and wrote an early church writing called the epistle of Barnabas. In chapter 15:3-5 of the epistle attributed to him, he writes:

> *"Of the Sabbath He speaketh in the beginning of the creation; And God made the works of His hands in six days, and He ended on the seventh day, and rested on it, and He hallowed it. Give heed, children, what this meaneth; He ended in six days. He meaneth this, that in six thousand years the Lord shall bring all things to an end; for the day with Him signifyeth a thousand years; and this He himself beareth me witness, saying; Behold, the day of the Lord shall be as a thousand years. Therefore, children, in six days, that is in six thousand years, everything shall come to an end. And He rested on the seventh day. this He meaneth; when His Son shall come, and shall abolish the time of the Lawless One, and shall judge the ungodly, and shall change the sun and the moon and the stars, then shall he truly rest on the seventh day."*

In case you were not able to follow his statements. He is relating the six days of creation to a time ordained by the authority of God to be the time of man and the rule of the "lawless one." Likewise, the seventh day of rest refers to the coming millennial kingdom. Barnabas is stating that mankind will have six thousand years. The seventh day will be the one-thousand-year reign of Jesus. For those who are familiar, it refers to the millennial kingdom. I find this insightful and hopeful.

Patience of God

Peter also writes of the timelessness of God, including the idea of the patience of God toward mankind in 2 Peter 3:8-9, "⁸ But do not forget this one thing, dear friends: With the Lord, a day is like a thousand years, and a thousand years are like a day. ⁹ The Lord is not slow in keeping his promise, as some understand slowness. Instead, He is patient with you, not wanting anyone to perish, but everyone to come to repentance." The goal of this passage is to help us understand that the patience of God is for the benefit of the redemption of mankind.

Adam

Consider Adam. If the days of creation were indeed longer, then we would not be able to account for the age of Adam provided in scripture. We are told in Genesis that mankind was created on the sixth day. Adam was created on the sixth day, and the seventh day of rest followed. Yet we know according to Genesis 5:5 that "all of the days of Adam were 930 years". If the day were any period of time longer than the original length of a day, then Adam would presumably have been much older than he was. If each day of creation was equal to one thousand years and then changed to a 24 hours day, then Adam would have been much older. He would have been at least 1930 to 2930 years old, thousand years for the seventh day of rest, possibly a thousand years for the sixth day, depending on at which point in the day he was created, plus the additional 930 years that we have listed for his age. He was not.

Two Accounts

One of the other areas that seem to confuse people is that they believe that the Bible shows two accounts of creation and two accounts of the flood, but that is not the case. We are reading the "what" and the "How." First, we are told, "this is what God did." Then we are told, "this is how God did it." Not the genetics of how but a more detailed account. It is not two accounts, but one version is given in greater detail to increase our understanding of what occurred.

I mention these perspectives on Genesis because I am aware that some of you will disregard any further information that I may present when I say "creation." I am asking you to continue reading and to continue searching out scriptures.

mDNA

If you would like to see where science is starting to catch up with the Bible, I would recommend that you study mitochondrial DNA, mDNA, also known as mtDNA. One of the exciting aspects of DNA is that it demonstrates we all go back to one source for our DNA. One ancestorial couple. The mitochondrial DNA is the energy production center for a cell. Mitochondrial DNA is DNA that is only passed from the mother. It is maternal. The mDNA reveals two amazing truths. One is that there was a bottleneck in human history. The bottleneck occurred at the biblical timeline for the flood. It is mentioned in the account of Noah as recorded in the book of Genesis. The other thing that it demonstrates is evidence of three lines of mDNA that branched out from the time of this bottleneck. This would correlate to the wives of Ham, Shem, and Japheth. The sons of Noah. I have loved the time I have spent researching information such as this. This is an amazing area of study that humanity is beginning to understand, and I have probably spent too much time on this topic. I will not bore you with it now, but I recommend exploring it for yourself. I want you to own the answers you discover through your research. It would be easier for you to accept than to receive what I might provide.

All of this shows a young age for the earth at approximately six thousand years ago. The DNA bottleneck provides scientific evidence for the truth of the Bible and the flood that occurred. Regarding the flood, it is interesting that every culture has an account of the deluge. The accounts range in similarity to the Genesis account, but it is interesting that they exist. It would make sense that as Noah and his family came off the ark and began to repopulate the earth, their children taught this flood history. As the family grew and they spread over the earth, the account changed over time.

The account of the flood probably changed over time. Probably in the same way as the exercise where you have people sitting in a circle and telling a story into the ear of the person to your right. There was much change from the original account by the time the story gets back to the person who started it.

Some researchers believe that the biblical history of the flood was taken from earlier manuscripts provided by other cultures. I do not believe this to be the case. I believe the most accurate account would remain with the first family. Noah remained 350 years after the flood. He provides a detailed record of events before and after the flood. The incredible accuracy of this historical record is conveyed to us as we find it today in the Bible. We will talk more about Noah soon as there is much that was occurring during this time period.

The bottom line is this. God had the authority to create. God also has the power to create. By the counsel of his own will, He did create.

Chapter 4

AUTHORITY TO IMPART AUTHORITY:

This is an interesting aspect to consider when it comes to authority. God, who has all authority, can impart authority to others. We can understand this from our earlier example of the president deriving his authority from the people. In this case, God, who has all authority, can give authority over to others.

Since God is the one who maintains absolute authority, God can impart authority, and He does so for Adam and Eve. In Genesis 1:28, "God blessed them; and God said to them, "Be fruitful and multiply, and fill the earth, and subdue it; and **rule over** the fish of the sea and over the birds of the sky and over every living thing that moves on the earth." Adam and Eve now had the legal authority to reign over their world. To go forth and multiply, but also to go forth and **rule over** and subdue.

This rule is vitally important to understand because this authority was not to be long-lived. It only lasted until they disobeyed the clear direction that was given to them by God. Then they lost that authority, and it passed to another. The same statement given in Genesis 1:28 is also given to Noah after the flood In Genesis 9:1 but with a clear distinction. In Genesis 9:1, He tells them to be fruitful and multiply and fill the earth. He does not tell them that they will rule over it. This is a critical distinction because it reveals that something happened to humankind's previous authority.

I want to share with you a perspective based on the Word of God. Many people speculate when Satan could have fallen. Some say it happened many years, even thousands of years before Adam and Eve fell. I do not believe that this is so. At the end of each day of creation, we see that God saw what He had created and declared it was good. If it was good, it stands to reason that it was not bad and, therefore, not evil. At the end of the sixth day, He saw all that He had created and declared, Behold, it was "very good," Genesis 1:31. This means that the fall of Satan could not have yet happened.

Jesus is God

Speaking on creation, the passage we find in Colossians 1:16 reads,

> [16] *For by Him all things were created that are in heaven and that are on earth, visible and invisible, whether thrones or dominions or principalities or powers. All things were created through Him and for Him."*

The passage provides a great reveal. When comparing this passage with Genesis 1:1, "In the beginning God created…" The passage in Colossians talks about Jesus being the creator. So, if Jesus is the creator, what does that, according to scriptures, tell us about Jesus? If you answered God, then you are correct. Scriptures clearly teach that Jesus is God. Of course, the main thing for our purpose now is to see that creation included things in the heavenly places. He created the angelic forces too. This complete, complex creation was declared very good at the end of day six.

I love putting the puzzle pieces together and discovering the truth taught in the Bible. Read this passage from Ephesians in speaking of these principalities and powers. Ephesians 6 verse 12,

> *¹² For our struggle is not against flesh and blood, but against the rulers, against the powers, against the world forces of this darkness, against the spiritual forces of wickedness in the heavenly places.*

It seems to me that Jesus, God, created all things in those six days before resting and included spiritual beings too. We are not told of another time that creation occurred, just that Jesus created it all. Just for the sake of the creation argument, even if we were to say that they were created millennia before, at the end of the sixth day, it was all still "very good." So, it would stand to reason that the adversary, Lucifer, had not yet fallen. I would say that he, Satan, fell at the same time as Adam and Eve. This is particularly evident because of the judgment meted out to Satan at the time judgment was given to Adam and Eve.

So why do I mention the fall of Satan here? It is for this reason. All the authority that God gave to Adam and Eve to go forth and multiply, subdue, and rule, no longer applied. As we saw in Genesis 9, they were told to go forth and multiply, but something had changed as a result of the fall. The fall was that original act of rebellion against God. The first sin.

Here is what changed. All the **authority** that God had imparted to Adam and Eve had now passed on to another. All the authority that God had granted to them over this planet now belonged to Satan.

Satan is a word that means adversary. Satan was in opposition to God. He was an adversary of God. After the fall, these types of names were used for Satan. As we see in John 12:31, "and Now judgment is *upon* this world; now the **ruler of this world** will be cast out." Everything changed. All the authority that God gave to Adam and Eve passed over to Satan as a result of their sin. Sin severed their relationship with God, and at that very moment, Satan usurped their authority and became the ruler of this world.

At this point, we should talk about boundaries. Who is it that has the power to establish boundaries? It is the one who has authority.

Chapter 5

AUTHORITY TO IMPART BOUNDARIES:

Since God is the one who chose to create by the counsel of his own will, power, and authority, He, by all rights, has the authority to impose boundaries on his creation. My belief is that He did so to remind them that they were not independent of their creator. While they were given authority, their relationship with Him should remain primary. Ultimately their authority existed because of God. God gave it to them. I think in the same way, our government must remember that its authority is derived from the people. God wanted to remind them that their authority was given to them by Him. That is someone with greater authority.

This is what we see in the establishment of boundaries for Adam and Eve. God told Adam and Eve that everything he had created was for them. Why did He do this? Because mankind was the pinnacle of God's creation. Of man, we are told, He created his image uniquely. When God created mankind, He breathed into him the breath of life. While God created everything, we are told mankind was formed in the image of God.

While in seminary, we had some debate as to what the image of God means. Is it a spiritual implication? Is it an attitude of character? What is it? For me, I believe that we can overthink some of these things to a large degree. The main characteristic I believe scripture is referring to is that man was created as a tri-part being. This is in the likeness of God. God is presented in scripture as a triune God, evidenced in the Bible as Father, Son, and the Holy Spirit. We see scripture revealing this in passages such as 1 Thessalonians 5:23. Man is created as body, soul, and spirit. 1 Thessalonians 5:23 reads, *"Now may the God of peace Himself sanctify you entirely; and may your spirit and soul and body be preserved complete, without blame at the coming of our Lord Jesus Christ."* The Trinity is a little harder to grasp from Hebrews 4:12, I see it clearly, *"For the word of God is living and active and sharper than any two-edged sword and piercing as far as the division of soul and spirit, of both joints and marrow, and able to judge the thoughts and intentions of the heart."*

This passage in Hebrews is one of my favorite scriptures. I have preached full sermons on it. It is powerful for a deeper understanding of the Word of God. For our purposes at this time, we see distinction presented in a triune format spirit, body, and soul. It is presented in a way that reveals the power and authority of the Word of God. In brief, the separation between soul and spirit is the first distinction mentioned. The statement in and of itself would imply that the soul and spirit are not the same. To understand what we are taught, the segment separating the soul and the spirit refers to the spirit. The next section of joints and marrow focus on the flesh, while the third section focuses on the soul.

We see this distinction in reference to God in such passages as Matthew 28:19, "Go, therefore, and make disciples of all the nations, baptizing them in the name of the Father and the Son and the Holy Spirit."

I want to say that the word triune or trinity is not in the Bible. Cults are good at bringing this point out. Even Muslims who believe in the teaching of the Quran believe in Jesus. They just do not believe that He is God. While the word trinity is not in the Bible, that does not mean that it fails to teach the triune nature of God. There is a distinction.

I came in as the new pastor of a church where the previous pastor was still around the congregation. He stated to me that Jesus never claimed to be God. Yet, in passages such as John 14:9, we read, "Jesus said to him, "Have I been with you for so long a time, and *yet* you have not come to know Me, Philip? The one who has seen Me has seen the Father; how *can* you say, 'Show us the Father?'" Or even the Colossians 1:16 passage I mentioned earlier regarding creation provides clarity that Jesus is God.

Over the ages, we have devised theological words that people use to describe things like the tri-part nature of man or even God. A dichotomist, for example, would believe that man is a two-part being often expressed as body/soul and spirit. They believe the body and soul are one. I believe in a trichotomy view of body, soul, and spirit. We are again allowing scripture to interpret scripture. It is primarily through the body that mankind can relate to the physical world around us, which God created for us and placed us all within. The soul is where we find the seat of our emotions, mind, and will. We can connect to, have fellowship with, and learn to understand the creator through the spirit. Without the spirit, we could not grow to understand who God is. As we are taught in 1 Corinthians 2:14, "But a natural person does not accept the things of the Spirit of God, for they are foolishness to him; and he cannot understand them, because they are spiritually discerned."

Of God, the word Elohim is in the masculine plural. I mention the masculine form because I have heard it taught that God is a mother, not a father, because Elohim is in the feminine, but that is not true. In Hebrew plural, the feminine ends in (ot), whereas the masculine ends in (im). Genesis provides the name of Elohim for the name of God. This is the masculine form. Let alone the fact that God refers to himself as Father. Likewise, Jesus, in the Lord's prayer, begins with, "Our Father."

Regarding the plural, Hebrew has singular, dual, and plural. While single is self-evident, dual means two, usually used in reference to pairs, such as ears, eyes, etc., whereas plural means more than two.

In this case, three are Father, Son, and Holy Spirit. This does not mean there are three Gods. But one God who is Father, Son, and Holy Spirit. Do you find that confusing? You would not be the first. Think of it from the perspective that you are one person uniquely created as a triune being. You are body, soul, and spirit, yet one person. My spirit is not my flesh or soul. My flesh is not my spirit or soul. My soul is not my spirit or flesh, yet I am uniquely created as one person. This does not accurately reflect the image of God but reveals that we are created in his image as a triune being.

People have often tried to use various created items to express the image of God in an effort to explain the Trinity, such as the egg, which is one egg uniquely expressed as yolk, white, and shell, yet it is only one egg. This can lead to what is called modalism. Modalism is a form of heresy inaccurately explaining the trinity and would teach that God is a single person who manifests himself in these three different forms or modes. This does not accurately express the trinity. The trinity is expressing that we have only one God who eternally exists as plural. God the Father, the Son, and the Holy Spirit are all coequal in attribute and of one mind. In complete unity.

We can see this clarity of distinction best in Matthew 3:16-17,

> *"After being baptized, Jesus came up immediately from the water; and behold, the heavens were opened, and he saw the Spirit of God descending as a dove and [ii]lighting on Him, and behold, a voice out of the heavens said, "This is My beloved Son, in whom I am well-pleased."*

In Deuteronomy 6:4, it reads, "Sh'ma Yisrael Adonai Eloheinu Adonai Eḥad: "Hear, **O** Israel: the LORD is **our God**, the LORD is **One**." Adonai is in the single, whereas Elohim is in the plural. Eloheinu is in what is called the plural, first-person possessive. While first-person possessive is used in Deuteronomy, in Genesis, it is Elohim. You only need to read the English translation: "Hear, **O** Israel: the LORD is **our God**, the LORD is **One**" to understand.

He, God, "created" everything. But when it comes to man, we are told something different, more unique. Of man, we are told, he said in Genesis 1:26-27,

> *"Then God said, "Let Us make man in Our image, according to Our likeness; and let them rule over the fish of the sea and over the birds of the sky and over the cattle and over all the earth, and over every creeping thing that creeps on the earth." God created man in His own image, in the image of God, He created him; male and female, He created them."*

And in Genesis 2:7, we read, "Then the LORD God formed man of dust from the ground and breathed into his nostrils the breath of life, and man became a living being." He even made a garden for them and placed them in it.

He created the garden with everything they could possibly need or desire. In this garden, He included a tree of life and a tree of the knowledge of good and evil. He gave them this one boundary (I know, finally back to the topic of boundary). He told them they could do anything but eat of the tree of the knowledge of good and evil. For a time, mankind followed this counsel. But it did not last. When we talk about what occurred, there are some things we should consider. First, Adam was given this directive to not eat of the tree prior to the creation of Eve. Genesis 2:15-17 reads,

"Then the LORD God took the man and put him into the garden of Eden to cultivate it and keep it. The LORD God commanded the man, saying, "From any tree of the garden you may eat freely; but from

the tree of the knowledge of good and evil you shall not eat, for in the day that you eat from it you will surely die."

Eve was not created based on the scriptures when Adam was given this instruction. It is only after that God created Eve, in verse 21. Adam passed on the teaching of the acceptable boundaries to Eve. While we do not have an account of the conversation, I believe it could have gone something like, "Of this tree, the tree of the knowledge of good and evil you shall not eat, for in the day you eat of it, you will surely die. You know what, Eve, we should not even touch it!" If this was the case, Adam made a vital mistake of adding to the Words that God had spoken. Adding to God's word is never a good idea. This conversation is only speculation on my part. I believe it occurred somewhat like this because when Eve encountered the serpent, she answered the serpent by saying, "From the fruit of the trees of the garden we may eat; ³ but from the fruit of the tree, which is in the middle of the garden, God has said, 'You shall not eat from it or touch it, or you will die." Genesis 3:2-3. She added to the words that God had spoken. As far as we have revealed to us, God never said that. Once again, I know it is just an assumption on my part, but I believe the addition came from Adam, and it set Eve up for failure. She thought that she would die if she ate from it or even touched it.

Satan rejoices when we add or take away from the Word of God. It allows him room to maneuver, just as it did here. I can almost see him reaching up to touch the fruit as he tells her, "You shall not surely die" (Genesis 3:4). When she saw that he touched it and did not die, it gave credibility to his deception. She touched it too and did not die. So maybe the serpent was right. Maybe he was telling the truth, and God was withholding something valuable from them. She touched it, somewhat like you might touch a stove, to see if it was hot. She placed her hand on it, and she did not die. She picked it, and did not die. So why not eat from it too?

One of the most vital truths we can understand here is that this moment was the beginning of spiritual warfare that still exists today. We cannot overlook that reality. The enemy is still trying to get humanity to violate the precepts of God. He is still trying to get us to add or take away from the Word of God, and he uses that to gain access into the lives of people today to trap them into the bondage of sin and to turn them away from God.

Chapter 6

AUTHORITY USURPED:

Several scriptures are historically interpreted as being about Satan. One of these passages is found in the book of Isaiah, chapter 14. While it is frequently understood to be referring to Satan, as you will see, some say it is possible to also refer to the earthly king of Babylon. The passage is in the book of Isaiah 14:12-15,

> [12] *"How you have fallen from heaven,*
> *O star of the morning, son of the dawn!*
> *You have been cut down to the earth,*
> *You who have weakened the nations!*
> [13] *"But you said in your heart,*
> *'**I will** ascend to heaven;*
> ***I will** raise my throne above the stars of God,*
> *And **I will** sit on the mount of assembly*
> *In the recesses of the north.*
> [14] *'**I will** ascend above the heights of the clouds;*
> ***I will** make myself like the Most High.'*
> [15] *"Nevertheless you will be thrust down to Sheol,*
> *To the recesses of the pit.*

We find insight in the book of Ezekiel too. In Ezekiel 28:12-18, We read.

> "You had the seal of perfection, Full of wisdom and perfect in beauty." You were in Eden, the garden of God; Every precious stone was your covering:
> The ruby, the topaz and the diamond; The beryl, the onyx and the jasper;
> The lapis lazuli, the turquoise and the emerald; And the gold, the workmanship of your settings and sockets, Was in you. On the day that you were created
> They were prepared "You were the anointed cherub who covers,
> And I placed you there. You were on the holy mountain of God;
> You walked in the midst of the stones of fire. "You were blameless in your ways
> From the day you were created Until unrighteousness was found in you.
> "By the abundance of your trade You were internally filled with violence,
> And you sinned; Therefore I have cast you as profane From the mountain of God.
> And I have destroyed you, O covering cherub, From the midst of the stones of fire. "Your heart was lifted up because of your beauty; You corrupted your wisdom by reason of your splendor. I cast you to the ground"

Of course, we know that no earthly King fell from heaven or existed in Eden, the garden of God. So from just those statements, we can understand this was not merely referring to a person.

Many passages reveal more about the covering angels, such as Hebrews 9:1-5, Exodus 25:17-22, Hebrews 9:23-24, 1 Kings 6:19-28, and others. The main point is that the Cherub mentioned in Ezekiel is no longer holding that position he once occupied. He has been cast down. Isaiah 14:12 once again reads, "How you are fallen from heaven,

O Day Star, son of Dawn! How you are cut down to the ground, you who laid the nations low! In Revelation 12:4, "And the great dragon was thrown down, that ancient serpent, which is called the devil and Satan, the deceiver of the whole world—he was thrown down to the earth, and his angels were thrown down with him." Luke 10:18, "And he said to them, "I saw Satan fall like lightning from heaven." In Revelation 20:2, speaking of things to come, we read, "And he seized the dragon, that ancient serpent, who is the devil and Satan."

We know from the mentioned passages that the covering angel would dwell in the holiest of holies, in the throne room of God. As is a common understanding, we can assume that this angel who fell was Lucifer, to become known as Satan. In Luke 10:18, "[18] And He said to them, "I was watching Satan fall from heaven like lightning." In 1 Timothy 3:5-6, speaking of leadership in the church, we read, "[6] *and* not a new convert so that he will not become conceited and fall into the condemnation incurred by the devil." From his grand position, Satan became arrogant and thought more highly of himself than he ought, and this pride led him down a path of rebellion against God.

Satan is a title meaning adversary, his name is Lucifer, and he is one of three angels mentioned by name in scripture. Yes, I know other writings that mention other angels, like Raphael in the apocryphal book of Tobit. I do not consider the apocryphal books to be inspired works due to inconsistencies with the rest of the scripture. Let alone the inconsistent nature of Raphael himself. Remember, it is always best to let scripture interpret scripture. In the Bible, we see three angels we consider archangels, which are mentioned by name: Michael, Gabriel, and Lucifer. Lucifer was the guardian of the throne room of God. He was the most beautiful of angels. He became prideful and, as a result, desired to be god himself. He desired to establish his own kingdom and rule. Reread the "I" statements above in Isaiah 14:12-15. This is where the problems began.

I want us to notice; however, where it all started, it is recorded in Isaiah 14:13, "Because you said in your heart." Sin always begins in the heart before it is manifested in our actions. I would even caution us with the reality that it begins with the mind before it takes hold in the heart.

Battlefield of the Mind:

The mind itself is the battlefield on which we fight. That is why we should heed the instruction of Psalm 119:11, in which David writes, "Your word I have treasured in my heart, That I may not sin against You." The battlefield is the mind, and as temptation comes into our mind, we battle it with scripture that we have already learned, studied, memorized, and hidden away in our hearts. This prior work is the primary means of experiencing victory as we walk through this world.

Romans 12:1-2 teaches us,

> "Therefore I urge you, brethren, by the mercies of God, to present your bodies a living and holy sacrifice, acceptable to God, *which is* your spiritual service of worship. ²And do not be conformed to this world, but be transformed by the **renewing of your mind**, so that you may prove what the will of God is, that which is good and acceptable and perfect.

From what we have already read, it is easy for us to recognize that God has not created us to be robots. God has created us with free will. But with our freedom comes accountability. We are responsible for our actions. If I break the law, then I may be held accountable to the law and suffer the consequences that the law may require. This is true in the spiritual realm too. We are responsible and accountable for our choices and bear the responsibility for the consequences that may come as a result of our choices.

If it were not for God's grace, there would be no hope for any of us. Our goal as believers is to walk not after the flesh but after the spirit of God, which indwells us. This is where the warfare comes in. We are accustomed to walking by the flesh and seeing things from the perspective of the flesh as it relates to the world around us. Once we come to know Jesus as Lord and Savior, sin has been dealt with, and we are quickened or made alive in our spirit. Our spirit is joined with the spirit of God, as we were designed to be. His spirit gives life to our spirit. We are filled with the spirit of God.

The Shekinah glory refers to the presence of God dwelling with his people. It is used of Israel leaving Egypt being led by the pillar of cloud or fire. Or the presence of God indwelling the temple in the holy of holies, where only the high priest could go. This same spirit indwells every person who has come by faith to Jesus, who has had their sin debt paid and received the holy spirit as a pledge of our inheritance. Romans 8:9 speaks of this indwelling, "However, you are not in the flesh but in the Spirit, if indeed the Spirit of God dwells in you."

Prior to knowing Jesus and being filled with the spirit, the only way to view the world was through the flesh. Because we have been filled with the spirit of God, we can begin to see things from the perspective of the spirit. How effective we become at this is a matter of growth. We have to learn to walk under the authority of the spirit rather than the authority of the flesh. In other words, we learn to live and make choices by understanding the will of God through the spirit of God who indwells us, rather than from the perspective of the flesh, as we once did.

Learning to walk in the spirit means to walk by the counsel and guidance of the spirit of God. Walking in this way is essential if we are going to start living in victory over the flesh and the things of the world. If we could successfully walk by the spirit of God one hundred percent of the time, we would never sin. This is what we are taught in passages such as Galatians 5:16, "But I say, walk by the Spirit, and you will not carry out the desire of the flesh." But it is difficult. The flesh gets in the way. It still wants to remain in control. Galatians 5:17 reads, "For the desire of the flesh is against the Spirit, and the Spirit against the flesh;

for these are in opposition to one another, in order to keep you from doing whatever you want." Or in Romans 8:5, "For those who are in accord with the flesh set their minds on the things of the flesh, but those who are in accord with the Spirit, the things of the Spirit." The difficulty is that we continue to live in this world too. Our flesh relates to the world and continually seeks to pull us back into the world. It is also the desire of the enemy of God to keep us walking under the authority of our flesh so that we are ineffective for God. However, while we find ourselves in the world, we are not of the world. Those who are redeemed are no longer subjects of the adversary, trapped by the bondage of sin. We are no longer under his authority. We are under the authority of Jesus. He may have usurped the authority given to Adam and Eve and won a kingdom for himself, but Jesus reclaims those who are lost and brings them under his authority.

Chapter 7

AUTHORITY TO IMPART JUDGMENT:

The serpent operating through his free will came into the garden, having devised a plan. He knew that God had given mankind authority over this world and everything in it. God gave them a kingdom to rule over. He also knew that they were given a boundary and, with that boundary, stated consequences.

Eve may have had good intentions. The food looked good to eat and had the added benefit of making one wise. The serpent did not die when he touched it, and she did not die when she touched it, so maybe she would not really die if she ate of it. Being deceived by Satan, she took and ate and gave it to her husband, who, according to Genesis 2:6, was "<u>with her</u>," and he ate. Notice she did not have to go somewhere to get her husband. Chances are he was right there the whole time listening to the conversation. Who knows why he did not step up and say something? He knew better than to believe the lie. Maybe it was due to the astonishment that a serpent was speaking. Perhaps simply because he chose his wife over obedience to God, whatever the reason, Eve may have been deceived, but Adam made a conscious choice to rebel against the command of God and violated the one boundary that God had given. He chose to sin.

There is much in scripture on this topic, but for now, I would have us simply understand what we are told in Romans 5:12, "[12] Therefore, just as through one man sin entered into the world, and death through sin, and so death spread to all men because all sinned" The sin of the man and the woman is attributed to the choice the man had made. Judgment falls upon them all. They all sinned and had their own consequence for their actions. Satan sinned. Adam sinned, and Eve sinned. They all fell. But that sinful choice that condemned all of mankind fell on the shoulders of Adam. Once again, Eve was deceived, but Adam made a choice.

God is the creator and has all authority. He has the authority to set boundaries. He has the authority to impart judgment due to sin.

The next thing we need to understand in the development of this topic is that God is God. One of his attributes is omniscience. In other words, He is all-knowing. This attribute of God is taught in many places in the Bible, such as in Psalm 139:4, where it says, "Even before a word was formed on my tongue, behold oh Lord, you know it all."

As I mentioned in the opening, out of all the possible ways in which God could have proceeded, knowing we were going to rebel and fall into sin, He set a plan into motion to rescue or save us before the very foundation of the world was laid. Ephesians 1:4 reads, "just as He chose us in Him before the foundation of the world, that we would be holy and blameless."

Because God is God and He knows all, it is important for us to understand what is occurring in this Genesis passage. We see God coming into the garden and asking, "Adam, Eve, where are you?" Genesis 3:9. "Did you eat of the tree I told you not to eat thereof?" Genesis 3:11?

He is God. He is Omniscient. He knew where they were, and He knew what they did. So, we must ask, why is this in my Bible? Why did God approach the situation in such a way? He knew what happened.

These questions were asked to show them and to show us that something had happened. Something uniquely changed in their relationship. Not only were they aware of things they were not previously aware of, but they were also aware that something had happened to their relationship with God.

Remember the trichotomy view of the creation of man. We were created in the image of God as body, soul, and spirit. It is important to understand that God created us with life. We were alive body, soul, and in the spirit. Death was never God's intended plan. Death became a reality as a result of sin. It was the inevitable result of sin. Now we see the truth of what God had forewarned them had come to pass. God said in Genesis 2:17, "for in the day you eat of it you shall surely die." They ate, and they died, right then, at that very moment, in the indwelling of the spirit of God. They still had a spirit, but sin had severed their relationship with God. They were now dead in the spirit, and their spirit no longer had the personal, intimate connection with God that they previously experienced. The relationship had changed.

Prior to their falling into the temptation and committing sin, they were alive in the body, soul, and spirit. Now, as a result of sin, death entered in. They were now body, soul, and dead in the spirit. Sin, which is always rebellion against God, had entered in, and they were now experiencing the consequence. Notice that they knew something had changed before God came into the garden. They were hiding, making clothing with fig leaves. They felt the very real sense of guilt and shame that sin will always bring.

Along with the spiritual death that occurred, it is also at this point that the physical degeneration of the human body began too. Remember that neither the death of the body nor the spirit was ever God's desire. This happened as a result of sin. It was the fault of man, not of God. Death came about as a result of sin. Sin came about as a result of choice.

While God did not want this to happen, He knew it was going to happen. As I mentioned, Ephesians 1:4 reads, "Just as He chose us in Him before the foundation of the world, that we would be holy and blameless before Him." God already has a plan to restore mankind from the consequences of death that sin brought about.

To be clear, the first state of man was the body, soul, and alive in the spirit. The second state that occurs is degeneration of the body, soul, and dead in the spirit. This event, which I would deem "the birth of death," is commonly called the fall or the fall of man. It speaks of the consequence of sin severing the relationship with God at the most intimate level, spiritual.

Theological rabbit trail

Administration Oversight

Allow me to rabbit trail (again) for a moment. There was such a dramatic change in the way we related to God that theologians had given it several names. In simple terms, it is in the administration of the way that God works with mankind. One is called a dispensational view, and another is from a covenantal view. For the dispensationalist, the fall moves us out of the dispensation of Innocence. From a covenantal perspective, it moved us out of the Adamic covenant (which is sometimes considered as two parts. The first was the Edenic covenant followed by the Adamic covenant).

Without opening up a full discourse on the subject, the distinction between the two, put simply, is this; a covenant (diatheke) is an agreement God makes with mankind. If you do this, then I will do this. It is based on a condition. God has his part, and we have our part. Whereas a dispensation (oikonomia, Greek) is a form of administration, management, or stewardship. I believe they have more in common than many would care to believe, and I do not believe they necessarily need to exist as one or the other. Both terms are used in the Bible. The Old and New Testaments, as an example, are the Old and New Covenants.

I open this door because there is controversy in the Christian church about such things. Personally, I think we cause far too much division over a variety of theological issues rather than building unity in the church that the Word of God calls us to. While this is not a treatise on the distinctions, I want us to consider the work of God from one other perspective.

As previously discussed, we have a God who is triune. Let me ask you a question. What is it that we were told God the Father did when He finished the work of creation? In Genesis 2:3, we read, Then God blessed the seventh day and sanctified it because in it He **rested** from all of the work which God had created and made. What we are told is that God rested. Some people have the view that God just wound things up and stepped back and left it to run on its own. They believe we have so much evil in the world because God left us on our own. Essentially, they think He created and abandoned his creation. We must again understand that authority over this world has changed. In the fall, the world became under the authority of the adversary, Satan. When God the Father rested on the seventh day does not mean that his work with his creation ended there. It did not end there.

Over the years, I have seen the reference to the appearance of God visiting mankind change, such as when He walked with Abraham in Genesis chapter 18. He appeared with two angels and spoke to and ate with Abraham. Accounts like this used to be referred to as a theophany. Theophany is a word derived from the Greek meaning "the appearance or manifestation of God to humankind." It has since become what we call a Christophany. A Christophany means the "appearance of Jesus" before his incarnation, such as Melchizedek, whom you can read about in Genesis 14:18. I believe the term Christophany is more accurate.

With that in mind, we have the Father resting on the seventh day after the creation of all things. This is not saying that God the Father is not involved, but simply to imply that the primary role after He rested was carried forth by God, the Son. The torch was passed. I want to add that it, of course, does not suggest that the Holy Spirit nor Jesus had anything to do with creation. We have already come to understand that Jesus was intricately involved. Again from Colossians 1:15-16,

> "He is the image of the invisible God, the firstborn of all creation. For by Him all things were created, both in the heavens and on earth, visible and invisible, whether thrones or dominions or rulers or authorities—all things have been created through Him and for Him."

Likewise, we are told in Genesis 1:2, "the Spirit of God was moving over the surface of the waters." So the Spirit was there and uniquely involved in creation too. The whole of the Trinity, God, was involved in the creative event.

When we read that God rested, it does not mean that God needed to rest or that the father ceased all action. I believe we are being told that God the Father had the primary administrative role up to this point, and the next work with humanity after the fall was taken on by God the Son. The primary role of Jesus lasted until his ascension. As we are told in Mark 16:19, "…when the Lord Jesus had spoken to them, He was received up into heaven and sat down at the right hand of God." Since that time, the Holy Spirit has taken on the primary role of working for the salvation of mankind. The Father has rested, the Son sat down, rested, and now the torch was passed to the Holy Spirit who goes into the world convicting man of sin righteousness and the coming judgment. John 16:7-10 reads,

> [7] But I tell you the truth, it is to your advantage that I go away; for if I do not go away, the Helper will not come to you; but if I go, I will send Him to you. [8] And He, when He comes, will convict the world concerning sin and righteousness and judgment; [9] concerning sin, because they do not believe in Me; [10] and concerning

righteousness, because I go to the Father and you no longer see Me."

It becomes incredible and exciting when you start to put some of these pieces together and begin to understand the bigger picture of what God has been doing throughout history. You can start to see the sovereign authority of God and his work in the world in order to bring about the redemption of fallen mankind.

Back to the Authority to impart judgment.

Now that we have laid more groundwork, let us turn our attention back to God's judgment through his sovereign authority on the day the fall occurred.

In Genesis 3, his judgment begins with the serpent. The lack of personal accountability we read through this section was astounding as God questioned Adam and Eve. When God asked Adam what happened, he said, "the woman you gave me." Essentially, he admitted that he listened to his wife rather than listening to the Lord without necessarily meaning to admit it. He also potentially had an accusatory tone toward God, saying, "The woman whom YOU gave me." (emphasis and speculation mine). Yet, Eve did the same thing. She blamed the serpent. "The serpent deceived me." God did not even ask the serpent. He simply declared, "Because you have done this." God knew where all of this had begun. Then He proceeded to pronounce judgment. God is sovereign and has the authority to pronounce judgment.

The most relevant part of the condemnation of Satan was when He stated that He would put enmity between him and the woman. Between his seed and her seed. Genesis 3:15, "And I will put enmity between you and the woman, and between your seed and her Seed; He shall bruise you on the head, And you shall bruise Him on the heel." In the movie "The Passion of Christ" (2004), Mel Gibson portrayed this beautifully as Jesus, in the garden of Gethsemane, stomped on the head of the serpent.

This judgment and the subsequent mention of the seed of the woman is called the protoevangelium. This is a compound of two words, proto -meaning first, and evangelion -meaning good news. It is the first mention of the fact that God has a plan of salvation for us. God has a plan to redeem mankind from the spiritual death that resulted from sin, and, ultimately, the new physical life at the resurrection to come.

God pronounced judgment on the serpent, on Satan. One of the main reasons we see the mention of the protoevangelium here is because God is saying to Satan that all of his scheming, manipulation, and deceit will come to nothing. It does not matter what he thought he was going to achieve because God has a plan more significant than the devil's schemes.

Of course, we have already learned from our Ezekiel 28 passage that Satan is a created being, "On the day *you were created*. " It also reveals to us that God is greater than Satan, has greater authority than Satan, and greater power than Satan. As believers, this world and its wickedness can become overwhelming at times. We must remember that God is in ultimate control, and all of God's plans will be carried out according to his design, according to HIS AUTHORITY.

Satan's Plan to Usurp Authority

We must understand that Satan wanted to usurp God and establish his own kingdom. He wanted to play God. Satan wanted to be God. He knew that by causing mankind to disobey God, their sin would separate them from God. He also knew that God gave Adam and Eve (humans) authority over this world and everything in it.

Lucifer also understood that if he could cut them off from God, he would be able to take over. If he could separate them from God, he, being a powerful spiritual being, could control what God had given them. They had died spiritually. Satan was cut off, and mankind was cut off. Both of these relationships had been impacted by sin. They had been severed. By choosing obedience to Satan rather than God, all authority that had been given to Adam and Eve passed to Satan. They made a choice to trust him, follow him, and believe him rather than God. Yes, I know that I am pounding this concept in here. Scripture teaches in Romans 6:16, "Do you not know that *the one* to whom you present yourselves *as* slaves for obedience, you are slaves of *that same one* whom you obey, either of sin resulting in death, or of obedience resulting in righteousness."

Once again, after the fall, we read names used for Satan like "Ruler of this world, in John 14:30. Or the Prince of this world in John 16:11. Satan usurped the authority given to Adam and Eve and took his position of authority as ruler over this world. This world is directly under Satan's control. This is his kingdom. The world was cast into spiritual darkness as a result of the fall. When Adam and Eve died in the indwelling of the spirit of God, Satan, a fallen angelic being, became the world's ruler. Now we can understand why after the flood in the days of Noah (Genesis 9:1), the command to "Rule over" was not reinstated.

We see this authority of Satan clearly in the temptation of Jesus, particularly in Mark 4:8, "Again, the devil took Him to a very high mountain and showed Him all the kingdoms of the world and their splendor. [9] "All this I will give you," he said, "if you will bow down and worship me." Satan actually had authority over this kingdom and had the authority to hand it over to Jesus.

For clarity, I want to be a little redundant in that I often hear people ask questions like, "If there is a God, then why do these bad things happen?" Now you know. It is because of the ruler of this world. Satan has a legal claim to this world and legal authority over it. We humans are not the only ones who feel the subjection to the adversary. Romans 8:22, for example, tells us that "ALL creation groans." The whole earth was impacted by the fall.

The whole world was cast into spiritual darkness under a wicked and evil ruler who, in his own pridefulness, rejected the love of God and chose to rebel. The world is still in spiritual darkness to this day. The usurper is still in authority in this world. As we look around at the world's condition, that is obvious. While hope has existed since the first mention of God's plan for our salvation in Genesis 3:15, this hope was made manifest and carried out in Jesus.

Chapter 8

THE AUTHORITY OF JESUS

Remember what Jesus said in Matthew 28:18, "¹⁸ And Jesus came up and spoke to them, saying, "All authority has been given to Me in heaven and on earth." Jesus had regained authority over the world. The enemy had been defeated. However, judgment has yet to be carried out. The world still operates under the authority of Satan. However, something has dramatically changed. Satan thought he could show Jesus an easy way out. Jesus could have accepted the offer to receive the kingdom of earth from Satan but at the expense of obedience to God the Father. Jesus, God the Son, is not less than God the Father, but He subjected Himself for a little while during his time living on the earth. Philippians 2:8 reads, "And being found in the fashion of a man, He humbled Himself and became obedient unto death—even the death of the cross." Hebrews 2:9 reads, "But we do see Him who was made for a little while lower than the angels, namely, Jesus, because of the suffering of death crowned with glory and honor, so that by the grace of God He might taste death for everyone."

When we can understand these truths, it changes our worldview. It changes how we understand what we see occurring around us, even now on the political stage. We must move from having a secular worldview to developing a biblical worldview. We must seek to understand the world through the lens of the Bible. When we do, everything falls into place, and it all begins to make perfect sense to us. As we become disciples of scripture and under the leadership of the Spirit of God and the teachers God places before us, we discover growth. This growth is part of the process of developing a biblical worldview.

The question you may ask now is why does God delay in holding off the judgment on Satan. If Jesus now has all authority, why is He waiting? What a great question, The simple answer is found in passages such as 2 Peter 3:9, "The Lord is not slow about His promise, as some count slowness, but is patient toward you, not willing for any to perish, but for all to come to repentance." Let's discuss the two kingdoms.

Two-Kingdoms

The world was cast into spiritual darkness, and we were all citizens of the kingdom of darkness. By faith, we find redemption through Jesus and come into this relationship with Him and are removed from under Satan's authority and brought under the authority of Jesus. We now have a kingdom of darkness and a Kingdom of light. We are now children of the Kingdom of light. 1 Peter 2:9 reads, "But you are A CHOSEN RACE, A royal PRIESTHOOD, A HOLY NATION, A PEOPLE FOR *God's* OWN POSSESSION, so that you may proclaim the excellencies of Him who has called you out of darkness into His marvelous light." As children of light, our goal is to expand our kingdom. We are told in Matthew 5:16, "Your light must shine before people in such a way that they may see your good works, and glorify your Father who is in heaven." Our purpose is to bring as many as we can from that kingdom of darkness into the kingdom of light. The only cost to enter this kingdom of light is faith. We are joined in the mission of Jesus for the salvation of others. There is no separating the life of the Christian from this kingdom's purpose. We are part of the kingdom of light.

When we talk about the authority of Jesus, we have to bring attention to the book of Mark. I will hit the highlights and recommend that

THE AUTHORITY OF JESUS

you read this in its entirety. When Jesus came out of the desert having refuted the temptations of Satan for forty days, the first thing He did was to begin preaching the gospel. "Repent and believe the gospel" was the message Jesus put forth in Mark 1:!5. He had just proved He was not going to bow to the one who had authority over this world. Immediately Mark begins talking about the authority of Jesus. He then begins recruiting his apostles and takes them with Him as he begins his work. As they went into Capernaum, the people were amazed at his teaching. We are told in Mark1:22 that he was teaching as one with authority.

I want to say that there is a lot of great truth to understand about Jesus in these passages, but since our focus is on authority, I will do my best to stay focused on this area. In the first area, we witness Jesus claiming authority over the demonically possessed man in Mark 1:24. This man was following Jesus. What business do we have with each other, Jesus of Nazareth? Have you come to destroy us? I know you are the holy one of God!" It is essential to recognize the reality of the spiritual realm again and that the demons recognized Jesus and knew He had the power to destroy them. Jesus takes authority over them and replies, "Be quiet and come out of him!" Jesus has authority over demons.

Next, we see Jesus enter the house of Simon, whose mother-in-law was sick with a fever. Jesus took her by the hand and raised her up, and she was healed. Jesus took authority over her sickness. Then we are told that word of these things was spreading, and the whole city came and gathered, and He healed the sick and cast out demons. His authority was not over one person sick or one person demon-possessed. He had absolute authority over all who were demon-possessed and all sickness. This is revealed in the coming section as they demonstrate his authority over illnesses that had no cure. Jesus healed a man of leprosy and another man who was paralyzed. The account of the paralytic man is a famous account you may have heard of because Jesus did more than heal the man. He told him his sins were forgiven.

The man's healing was to demonstrate that He indeed had the power to forgive sin, as evidenced in his ability to heal the man of his affliction. You can read about these things in Mark Chapters 1 and 2.

Jesus was already having trouble with the Jewish leaders. They were amazed at what He was doing, teaching as one with authority, healing the sick, casting out demons, and eating with sinners, so they followed Him to see what else He would do. Jesus was walking through a grain field on the Sabbath, and He and His disciples began picking the heads of the grain, which would be considered work that was not lawful on the Sabbath. The Pharisees quickly pointed this out, asking what He was doing and stating it was unlawful. Jesus in Mark 2:27 sums up his response by saying, "The Sabbath was created for man, not man for the Sabbath. So the Son of man is Lord even of the Sabbath," This authority is further demonstrated as they continue on the journey and enter the synagogue. Now the religious leaders were watching not just out of curiosity; they were watching to find out what else He was going to do to violate their law. In front of the synagogue congregation, Jesus heals a man with a withered hand. Jesus was literally confronting their religious norms. Not just to show that He had the power and authority to do so but as a demonstration of how they got so stuck in the letter of the law that they veered off track and missed the intent.

This demonstration of authority was before his death, burial, and resurrection. Jesus showed Satan in the temptation in the wilderness that he had no authority over Him. He then demonstrated his authority over the kingdom of Satan by healing the sick and casting out demons. He demonstrated that He had authority over the misguided religion, even those who claimed to represent Him. This is a great caution for us today.

We must seek to understand the Word in light of these truths. I have met many who have fallen into this headstrong attitude in their Christian faith that the Jews had in Jesus' day. They were seeking to follow the law according to the flesh. They looked to the law to save them rather than understand that it was designed to restrain the flesh and reveal they could not keep the law. Since they could not keep the law, salvation must come through some other means. Interestingly, the promise of salvation from the very beginning in Genesis was not through law but through the seed of the woman. It was the promise of a Messiah, a savior who would come to save their people from sin. Yet they got so stuck in the law that they missed this very Messiah in front of them. We have something today that they did not have back then. We have the indwelling of the Spirit of God. We are continually told in scripture to walk by the spirit. When Jesus died on the cross, and the veil in the temple of God was torn in two (Matthew 27:51), it demonstrated access to God. God was no longer closed off from us.

Chapter 9

THE SPIRITUAL REALM

The spiritual realm is as real as the physical realm. I would actually say that it is more real in that this world and everything in it is temporal and passing away. It is part of the kingdom of darkness where death lives, resulting from sin. In contrast, the kingdom of light is life eternal. This is not just an issue of the physical and spiritual worlds. Spiritual beings are in the kingdom of darkness of whom Satan sits as ruler. We find spiritual beings such as angels and demons in this spiritual realm.

Angels and Fallen angels

At the outset of this discussion, there are a few things I want you to understand. One is that spiritual warfare is real and does exist today. Two is that it is never to be our focus. We should always be aware of it, but our focus as believers is always to be Jesus. Three is that I want to talk about this reality without directing all of our attention to it. We need to understand more of this realm, but ultimately, we are talking about authority, not spiritual warfare. That will be a book for a different time.

Maybe you are familiar with this topic. I want you to know that I do not believe in anything like a "deliverance ministry." Once again, our focus is always to remain on Jesus. When these things come up, we deal with them, move on, and continue walking with our focus on Jesus. I am speaking more of the overt types of spiritual warfare here. There are many covert ways we battle every day, and with either, we need to develop spiritual discernment to understand them.

We have already talked about Satan. According to the scriptures, we can understand who he is and how he came to be. As with Lucifer, angels were created by God. Their primary realm of existence is in the spiritual realm. They can interact with this world we live in and with its inhabitants. Let us take a closer look at a few of the scriptures.

I want us to understand that potentially a third of the host of heaven followed Satan in his rebellion against God. However, no specific verse reveals this to us. It is speculation that exists because of a few passages. Revelation provides some of this knowledge for us and creates a clearer picture. Revelation 12:9 reveals, "And the great dragon was thrown down, the serpent of old who is called the devil and Satan, who deceives the whole world; he was thrown down to the earth, and his angels were thrown down with him. Revelation 12:3-4 reads, "Then another sign appeared in heaven: and behold, a great red dragon having seven heads and ten horns, and on his heads *were* seven diadems. ⁴ And his tail *swept away a third of the stars of heaven and threw them to the earth." This passage does not explicitly state that a third of the angels rebelled against God with Satan. However, it is typically understood that one-third of the angelic host joined him in the rebellion.

We have the names of three angels listed in scriptures, and these three are often considered archangels. Archangels itself (Greek, ἀρχάνγελος) is a word that means chief angel. In Hebrew, the transliteration is רַב־מַלְאָךְ *(rav-mal'ákh)*. Archangel is a term that essentially means the first position in rank or first position in the order. The word itself is only directly applied to Michael in Jude 1:9, "But Michael the archangel, when he disputed with the devil and argued about the body of Moses, did not dare pronounce against him an abusive judgment, but said, "The Lord rebuke you!" Michael is considered the warring angel from such passages as "Revelation 12:7-9

> "And there was war in heaven, Michael and his angels waging war with the dragon. The dragon and his angels waged war, and they were not strong enough, and there was no longer a place found for them in heaven. And the great dragon was thrown down, the serpent of old who is called the devil and Satan, who deceives the whole world; he was thrown down to the earth, and his angels were thrown down with him."

We do see the word, archangel, used in 1 Thessalonians 4:16 as well, where it reads, "For the Lord, Himself will descend from heaven with a shout, with the voice of *the* archangel and with the trumpet of God, and the dead in Christ will rise first." Typically it is Gabriel who is considered the messenger of God. He is the one who makes the announcements. Such as, in Luke 1:26-27, "Six months after Elizabeth had become pregnant, God sent the angel Gabriel to Nazareth, a city in Galilee. [27] The angel went to a virgin promised in marriage to a descendant of David named Joseph. The virgin's name was Mary." Or Gabriel speaking to Joseph in Luke 1:19, "The angel answered and said to him, "I am Gabriel, who stands in the presence of God." Michael became the warring angel, Gabriel, the messenger, and Lucifer, who was essentially the guardian angel of God's throne room, became Satan through his plotting and scheming.

The word Angelos is the word messenger. These angelic messengers have come in a few categories since the fall. Angels and Demons. These rebellious angels lost their heavenly abode along with Lucifer and were thrown out of heaven. These fallen angels are what today we call demons.

We know of Michael, Gabriel, and Lucifer. If each of these archangels is potentially in authority over a third of the host of heaven, then maybe the third under Satan's rule followed him in the rebellion. I am certainly not tied to which third or even a clear third, but I will state this is an inference on my part based on what we do know. There are no hard scriptural facts for which third of the angels rebelled or how many angels are actually in a third of the angels that make up the heavenly host.

We must understand that our battle is not against Satan alone. It is against the army of fallen angelic beings that are with him and under his authority. We have already looked at the temptation of Jesus, where Satan demonstrated his authority by offering the world's kingdoms to Jesus in Matthew 4:9. Since their fall, demons have set their purpose against God. Their goal is to destroy and cause pain. They want to pervert everything that God created. Like Satan, they will be judged for their sin. They continually seek to destroy those who have placed their faith in Jesus and to keep the lost in bondage to sin. They desire to stop the work of truth and righteousness in this fallen world. They want to put out the light.

Over the years, the fallen angels have been called demons. The word Demon comes from the word "daimon" in Greek, which can be translated as "genius." The name implies that demons are highly intelligent, which they are. It can also mean lessor spirit or evil spirit. So they are intelligent evil spirits and not to be taken lightly. I state this because I have seen people become arrogant and disrespectful in their attitude toward demons, and we should not. I can tell you from experience that I have been used by God many times in the area of spiritual warfare in my Christian walk. God has used me in dealing with those struggling with demon possession as well as Satanists. One aspect of demons you should be aware of is their relentless nature. They do not get tired and do not let up. We get tired, and we can give up after enduring a battle for so long. But direct attacks are only half of the battle. The enemy will use people close to you to cause chaos and even bring the battle to your family. It is heartbreaking and painful. The enemy will use people to lie about you and turn others against you.

It is important to understand that the enemy of God attacks where God is at work. The more intentional you are in your walk with Jesus, the brighter you shine as a light in this kingdom of darkness, and the more battle you will experience. But there is good news I will share soon.

I have heard people come up with interesting ideas about demons that are not necessarily according to the Bible. They may take one passage and run with it while forgetting others. We all do this from time to time as we grow in knowledge. It is part of the process of spiritual growth. But we must be careful to try to understand and see the big picture of scripture on any given topic, not just a single verse. We must also understand that we may not have remembered or considered a verse and always remain teachable on any given topic.

I heard a person make the statement that demons can only interact in this world if they possess a person. It does not even make sense if we think about it this critically. First, they would have to be able to move around in our world to get to the person they seek to possess. This ability to move in our world without possessing someone would refute that they need to be in someone first. We may talk about possession a bit later. Though once again, that may best be suited for another book.

The prophet Elisha was in the city of Dothan. The king of Aram came and surrounded the city. The servant of Elisha saw the army and was afraid, but Elisha prayed for the servant's eyes to be opened so that he might see the army of God that stood with Elisha. From 2 Kings 6:16-17, we read, "So he answered, "Do not fear, for those who are with us are more than those who are with them. Then Elisha prayed and said, "O LORD, I pray, open his eyes that he may see." And the LORD opened the servant's eyes, and he saw; and behold, the mountain was full of horses and chariots of fire all around Elisha. In the book of Job 4:15, we read, A spirit glided past my face, and the hair on my body stood on end. [16] It stopped, but I could not tell what it was. A form stood before my eyes, and I heard a hushed voice."

We can see from these passages that spiritual beings can be around us, and we just cannot see them. Also, Elisha's account shows that spiritual beings do not have to possess a person. There is no indication that any attributes have changed for fallen spiritual beings. It also shows that spiritual beings can speak and move so that we see them. Angels, as well as demons, are able to exist around us. We cannot normally see them looking with our normal human vision, though we may have our eyes opened at times. We should seek to discern their presence.

The fact that they can be all around us is easy for many to understand. We may not understand how this can be a reality, looking from a human perspective. It very well could be another plane of existence that crosses over to ours. Or, in some way, it allows them to operate in our world, allowing them to interact with our world and even influence us without our being aware of them. They can see us from their side, but we cannot see them from ours. As I have already mentioned, some people seem to live a little closer to the veil, and it is easier for them to experience the spiritual realm. While there is a spiritual gift called the gift of discernment, I would not say that I have that gift, but at times in my life, even before believing in Jesus, I had many personal experiences. In my personal experience, I have seen both what I would call demons and angels on several occasions.

I have always had these spiritual experiences in my life. Many people do not believe it because they have not experienced it for themselves. I will share one encounter with you from a time before I was even a believer in the Lord Jesus. I lived alone, and at one point, I became very sick. I had a bad fever and was sleeping on my couch. During the night, I woke up and saw a presence sitting on the edge of the sofa, looking at me. They were sitting on the arm of the couch and turned so that they could look at me. I felt at peace. I had no sense of fear at all, and I fell back to sleep. I did not wake up until morning, and my fever had broken. This presence, for whatever reason, was whitish, light in color. Another experience I had with this type of presence was after I was a believer in Christ. I woke up at night and saw a face over me, probably less than two feet away. Again, I felt at peace and fell comfortably to sleep. We were dealing with a lot of spiritual warfare at the time in a church I was pastoring in Montana.

I have also encountered dark forms, which I would call demons. On one occasion, my wife and I both woke up in the night as a dark presence passed over our bed. We felt it first, and that was what woke us up. Another night I woke up with a dark presence standing next to my bed. Without speaking, it told me it was going to afflict my son. It turned and went out, and about the time it would take to get to his room, my son cried out one time and was quiet again. He was three at the time. As you might imagine, we pray for our kids all the time.

In my walk with the Lord, I have dealt with people demonically possessed, and I have dealt with hardcore Satanists involved in human sacrifice. Someday I may write about the experiences I have had. Today, I want you to know that as a believer in the Lord Jesus and under the authority of the Lord Jesus, we are not under Satan's authority. We can act in the name of Jesus, in his authority to see those in bondage set free. Most importantly, they are free from the bondage of sin by turning from sin to the reality of grace and forgiveness in Jesus. We are told this directly in Galatians 5:1, "It was for freedom that Christ set us free; therefore keep standing firm and do not be subject again to a yoke of slavery."

Transitioning Authority

How I came to know Jesus

It was somewhere around the time I saw the presence sitting on the edge of my couch, I mentioned earlier, that I came to know Jesus as my Lord. As I stated previously, for me, my life was chaos. I felt it was out of control. My friends could not have seen its extent because, for most of them, their lives were the same as mine. I was carrying a heaviness with me. I had bounced between parents several times growing up, and I wasn't sure I really belonged anywhere. Having between parents, I found that when I would come back into the mix of friends, having had a gap of time in our relationships, I did not always feel a sense of belonging. I doubt they ever really knew how much I felt it.

I was one of these kids who made some stupid choices, and I was arrested at fifteen for stealing a car. We took a few that night, but I was arrested for the one I was caught driving. I had smoked marijuana and drank alcohol since I was ten. This was no different from anyone else, and my way of life seemed normal. It was the culture of sex, drugs, and rock and roll. I went to many concerts and looked for opportunities to party. The saving grace for me was that I had family around.

I wanted to take a few moments and tell you how I came to know the reality of Jesus in my life. I have already shared that my life was chaotic and that I had heard about Jesus when I was around seven at a Vacation Bible School program over the winter Christmas holiday. My parent divorced when I was ten years old and my father, finding himself with four kids to take care of, moved us to the city. My grandparents managed some apartments in the city, and they would be a help and support. As with many children, I bounced between my parents every few years. I lived a few years with one and then back to the other.

I will not go into all the stuff we got into because the salvation I have in Christ is greater than the sin I experienced. I do not want sin to be the focus. I will say that one of the best experiences was my time at my father's. Living in the city was much crazier than when I lived with my mother. We had extended family around. My two aunts also moved into the apartments along with my cousins. We had the opportunity to grow up together. We all varied in our level of craziness growing up, but we had a love for each other that mostly kept us somewhat grounded. However, life was filled with bad choices and heartache for most of us. For most of us, as with the rest of our neighborhood, we grew up with alcohol and other substances and all of the crazy that went along with that life.

We started to see some of our friends die. Sometimes by accident. One friend, while drunk, forgot to light the flame when he turned on a gas heater in his room, then passed out and died. Another made a willful decision to jump off a railroad trestle high above the road. I felt my time was coming, and to be honest, I would not have minded to a rather large degree.

One night about a month after my twenty-first birthday, completely sober, I was lying in bed and I was struck by the tragedy of my life and the choices I had made. I felt a different sort of heaviness, a sadness, an emptiness. I began to pray. I prayed to Jesus, asking for his help. I remember what they told me to say at that Vacation Bible School so long ago. In my own words, I told the Lord I knew I had made a mess of my life and wanted Him to forgive me. I asked Him to come into my life and help me make things right and do better. I had tears in my eyes, though my eyes were closed as I prayed.

The best way to explain what happened next is that it was like I was gone. Suddenly, I was standing in the middle of a big field; there was green grass, different colored flowers, and a tree line off to my right and another to my left. The tree line on the left turned to the right in front of me about two hundred yards up ahead. The sky was blue with some white clouds. It was beautiful. I remember wearing something white though I never looked down to see what I was wearing. I was too much in awe at the place itself. Walking in the field, I can still feel the grass under my bare feet.

I started to realize how I felt. I felt peaceful and content. I had never felt like this in my life before, and as soon as I started to grasp the feeling, I was gone. At first, I had no sensation in this second location where I found myself. It was absolute nothingness, darkness. There was no light, no sound, nothing.

You have probably heard people talk about seeing a bright white light. I saw this light. I probably would have never known that I was anywhere but for this bright white light that came out of the darkness from my right. I looked over toward it, and I was watching as someone was coming toward me out of the light. Instead of feeling peaceful and content, I felt afraid. The closer they got to me, the more scared I felt. The white light coming from behind the person caused them to appear as a dark silhouette. They got to about twelve to fifteen feet from me, I could tell it was a man, and I could just start to make out his features at the edges. The white light shining around the silhouette's darkness made the edges appear bluish. Then suddenly I was back in my bed. I opened my eyes, and as they did, they locked onto a shadow hovering up in the corner where the wall met the ceiling. I was wide awake, and my eyes were open. Without thinking about it, the words came out of my mouth, "Begone, my heart is with the Lord. Begone, my heart is with the Lord." I said that twice, and I watched the shadow as it shrank up and disappeared. I had no idea what had just happened. But I felt at peace and fell to sleep. That was my first experience exercising our authority as believers in the Lord Jesus over the spiritual forces of wickedness.

The next morning when I woke up, I knew I felt different, and I was. I have been free from drugs and alcohol ever since. I did, however, go out that next morning and steal a Bible. I knew I had asked Jesus for help, and I knew He had answered. I had a hunger in me I had not known before. I was hungry to learn. I started reading that stolen Bible for two to eight hours every day.

I tried to share what had happened to me with one of my cousins and many others. I don't think anyone really understood. I had a friend stop by with a six-pack and want to come in and drink. I told him he could come in but not the alcohol. He said, "Yeah, your cousin told me you saw God." Now 38 years later, I have shared my experience with many people on several continents.

All of that to say to you two things; the spiritual realm is real, and God will meet you where you are. He is not waiting for you to become something different. He is willing to meet you where you are and walk with you from there. Also, to say that spiritual warfare is real. It exists, and you are in the thick of it, whether you are aware of it or not. The enemy of God wants to keep you in the chains of spiritual bondage. His only hold on you is sin. Jesus came to set you free. He came to bring me from the kingdom of darkness into the kingdom of light. I have had a change of citizenship. I have no allegiance to the kingdom of darkness.

While I have had spiritual experiences before becoming a believer, it has been nothing like since I came to believe and trust in Jesus as my Lord. I may share more of these experiences if the Lord allows, but the one thing I want you to know is that as a follower of the Lord Jesus, you now have authority over these demons. And more importantly, you are no longer under the dominion of the Adversary. He no longer has authority over you. We live and walk and move and breathe under the authority of Jesus.

The fallen spiritual realm would prefer you not to notice them, let alone to understand your authority over them, which is a secret they do not want you to know. This is what we are taught in such passages as 1 John 4:4, "You are from God, little children, and have overcome them; because greater is He who is in you than he who is in the world."

Demons

Demons are spirits in the same way that angels are spirits. The only distinction is that demons have rebelled against God and have fallen, just as did Lucifer and just as fallen humankind. The difference is that we see no indication in scripture that there is any chance for redemption for the demon kind or Lucifer. I believe this is because they knew God and had a personal relationship with Him. Their relationship was beyond faith. Their relationship did not require faith because they knew God. Their relationship had come from direct experience, and they had real personal knowledge of God. We see dimly as through a smoked glass, and they knew Him face to face.

Demons as spirits are mighty. We should never forget that. It is only the Lord who restrains their acts of destruction. Likewise, we should never be arrogant and esteem too highly of ourselves in our battle against them. We are imperfect; fallen humans are redeemed only by a loving God's grace. It is never in our authority that we act. Scripture has a lot to say about demonic possession and deliverance. I will tell you that it is not an archaic principle of a less intelligent and superstitious society.

There exists what many believe to be a hierarchical order in the spiritual realm. In Ephesians 6:12, we read, "*12* For our struggle is not against flesh and blood, but against the rulers, against the powers, against the world forces of this darkness, against the spiritual *forces* of wickedness in the heavenly *places*." Some theologians create a hierarchical structure for the fallen spiritual forces from this passage. It may very well be. While I do believe there is a hierarchal structure, I am not sure this is it. More likely, it just imitates a structure. I believe this passage intends to move our minds in progression from seeing things as they are in this world to understanding the reality of the spiritual realm. Though changing our perspective, we might come to a greater understanding of the battle we face. That said, I believe that Satan is the one in authority and the rest of the demons have some destructive order of purpose they fall into. Again, it is important not to claim something in scripture that is unclear. It is better to state what scripture says and what you believe about it. I believe this (idea) is true because of what we read here. We cannot make a passage say something it does not intend to say. I would rather state what it says and tell you my belief and opinion on it. The distinction is important.

The above passage makes it easy to understand that we struggle not just against flesh and blood. There is a very real struggle that is taking place. The passage begins there and then moves us to understand that the battle is far greater. We battle with ourselves, humanity, and organized political and governmental structures. We struggle against world forces of darkness and then against spirits of wickedness in the heavenly places.

It is not my desire to focus on demonology in this book. But it is necessary to enter it a bit when discussing authority. Once again, we must understand that Satan has won legal authority over this world. He has authority over a host of fallen angels, who have come to be called demons over the generations. He also has authority over humanity until a person comes to know Jesus as Lord and Savior.

Seed of the Woman:

In talking about the wickedness of the Adversary and the authority that he has won over this world, casting the world into spiritual darkness, we must understand that God is still sovereign and ultimately in control. Remember, God is outside of time and knows the end from the beginning. He has his plan that has been woven throughout history, revealing itself for all to see. The only requirement is a willingness to look. We are even told in Matthew 7:7, "Ask, and it will be given to you; seek, and you will find; knock, and it will be opened to you." The knowledge of God and the fall events were transmitted from person to person; they knew what had occurred, and this knowledge was not lost.

At one point, while serving as a pastor of a church in Vaughn, Montana, I dug into the Bible and laid out the timeline and lineage of scripture. I followed verse by verse all the way back to Adam. I even made color-coded charts to lay out this information and each generation. One of the things I found interesting was that there was not a lot of time between Adam and Noah and then between Noah and Abraham. I discovered in this project that there existed only about 126 years between the death of Adam, who had lived 930 years, to Noah, born in about 1056. Noah's father, Lamech, was alive at the time of Adam. Lamech was born in the year 874. Adam died in the year 930, and they overlapped by 56 years. The dates I am providing are the simplest to understand, moving forward from the first day of creation. If the Adam and Noah overlap was not impressive enough for you, watch this. Noah died in about 2006, and Abraham was born in 1948. This overlap provides an overlap of 58 years! I find this amazing. It is entirely plausible to maintain an accurate history of these accounts in the same family system. Especially when accurate, historic verbal communication was an essential custom of the people.

A lot of history and world events happened over the amount of time covered. We are talking about the world's population growing and spreading out across the preflood earth. Scripture teaches us that the whole world grew wicked. It was so corrupt that God decided to save only Noah's family. He decided to destroy the rest of mankind and start over. I know this sounds like an incredibly drastic decision to make. There are reasons for this that you may or may not be ready to receive.

There was a reason for God to decide to destroy all of humankind. First, it has to do with the corruption of mankind that was plaguing the world at the time. This corruption occurred in two ways—the first was through the sinful choices that people were making. The second had to do with the corruption of humanity's genetic makeup. Remember the seed of the woman in Genesis 3:15, "And I will put enmity between you and the woman, and between your seed and her Seed; He shall bruise you on the head, and you shall bruise Him on the heel."

I want to start here by saying that there is controversy in the Christian church regarding the possibility that a genetic convolution could be even possible or that it could have in any way occurred. It is certainly a strange thought to consider that an angelic being could procreate with women. I am not God, and I leave all that is possible to Him. My goal is to study and make clear sense of what scripture has to say.

It is easy for us to read and see that the seed of the woman refers to the offspring that she would produce. Of course, in our Genesis 3 passage, this is referring to a specific seed, namely Jesus. This is evident by the use of He and His in the passage, "And I will put enmity between you and the woman, and between your offspring and hers; **He** will crush your head, and you will strike **His** heel." If we are to use this idea of her "seed" referring to an offspring that is to come in a future lineage of the woman, it will make sense then to apply the same principle to the reference of the seed of the serpent.

What are we talking about? In Genesis 6:1-5, prior to the flood, we read an interesting account that is not hard to comprehend, though it is hard to accept for some. It is interesting to note, as I mentioned previously, that no salvation for fallen angelic beings is ever introduced in scripture. Again, the reason, I believe, is that they have a personal relationship with God. They dwelt with Him in the spiritual realm, whereas we know of God. Not seeing God face to face, we come to believe in God by faith. Knowing who God is, having dwelt in his presence, they made a willful decision to rebel against God.

One of the fantastic things to understand here is that by making this statement of reference to "a seed" in Genesis 3:15, we see a revelation of the foreknowledge of God. As I mentioned before, this demonstrates for us that God knew in advance what Lucifer, Satan, was going to do. Lucifer may have thought he had won, but God revealed to him that all of his scheming and plans were laid bare before God. There was nothing hidden. What Satan planned for evil, God will work together for good. This is the very promise of God to us in Romans 8:28, "And we know that God causes all things to work together for good to those who love God, to those who are called according to *His* purpose."

Satan is an intelligent being. I believe his intelligence is far beyond what we humans have the capacity to understand. He understood what God was saying in Genesis 3, and he wanted to destroy the ability of the seed of the woman to bring about a Godly heir that would crush his head. An heir would ultimately end Satan's reign over this world. The promised "seed" would redeem fallen humanity and remove all who would come by faith out from under Satan's authority.

By regaining authority, Jesus could restore the world and those in it to its proper order.

While scripture does not mention a specific devised plan of Satan in this event, I personally believe (my speculation) that he orchestrated it. The account of the transgression is recorded for us. Most likely, Satan devised a plan to contaminate the woman's seed. We read about this account in Genesis 6:1-5,

> "Now it came about, when men began to multiply on the face of the land, and daughters were born to them, that the **sons of God** saw that the **daughters of men** were beautiful; and they took wives for themselves, whomever they chose. Then the LORD said, "My Spirit shall not strive with man forever, because he also is flesh; nevertheless, his days shall be one hundred and twenty years." The **Nephilim** were on the earth in those days, and also afterward, when the sons of God came in to the daughters of men, and they bore children to them. Those were the mighty men who were of old, men of renown. Then the LORD saw that the wickedness of man was great on the earth and that every intent of the thoughts of his heart was only evil continually."

Book of Enoch

There is a term we use known as apocryphal. It means something believed to be fictitious in nature, or at the very least not inspired God or written by men moved by the spirit. The book of Enoch falls into this category but may shed some light on ours topic. We find reference to this Genesis 6 account in the book of Enoch 6:1-4.

> "And it came to pass when the children of men had multiplied that in those days were born unto them

beautiful and comely daughters. And the angels, the children of the heaven, saw and lusted after them and said to one another: Come, let us choose us wives from among the children of men and beget us, children."

The idea is that in order to destroy the seed of the woman, demons, these spiritual beings (the sons of God, *bny ho'elohim*) came and procreated with women (the daughters of men). This is a disturbing thought. These offspring became men of renown. They were called Nephilim. The root of the word is Naphal, meaning fallen ones. They were uniquely different from the rest of humanity. We are told they were on the earth in those days and <u>afterward</u>. It is said that Goliath was one of such a son. They are mentioned after the flood in the book of Deuteronomy 2:10-11,

> [10] The Emites used to live there—a people strong and numerous, and as tall as the Anakites. [11] Like the Anakites, they too were considered Rephaites, but the Moabites called them Emites.

The Nephilim, having been sired by angelic, or fallen angelic beings, seems confirmed by other passages too. Jude 1:6, "And angels who did not keep their domain but abandoned their proper dwelling place, *these* He has kept in eternal restraints under darkness for the judgment of the great day." And from 2 Peter 2:4-5 we read,

> "For if God did not spare angels when they sinned but cast them into hell and committed them to pits of darkness, reserved for judgment; and did not spare the ancient world, but preserved Noah, a preacher of righteousness, with seven others, when He brought a flood upon the world of the ungodly."

Notice the progression from the angels who sinned to the destruction of the world through a flood.

To answer a question that may come to mind. Yes, the Nephilim were destroyed in flood with the rest of mankind. The only people who survived were Noah and His wife, their three sons, Ham, Shem, and Japheth, and the three sons' wives.

I believe from scripture that God chose Noah not just for his faith and righteousness but also for his purity, and that his wife and children were genetically pure too. They were children in the lineage of Adam and Eve. Their genetics were as God created them. The goal was to preserve the genetically pure race of humanity through whom the Messiah could come. The Messiah is, of course, the seed of the woman who would destroy the authority of the serpent of old. Now, while Noah, his wife, and his sons may have been pure, there appears to have been obvious genetic contamination in a few of their spouses. This genetic contamination of their wives allowed for a genetic mutation to have carried over post flood. Of Ham, Shem, and Japheth, I assume that Shem's wife was not genetically contaminated due to the promise of the Messiah's moving through his line.

I want to be very clear that this is not, in any way, talking about any issue of ethnicity. God creates every ethnic distinction for good and for His purpose and glory. Every ethnicity is completely equal and loved by God. He is a God of diversity in creation. One has only to look at the various birds, for example, to understand this truth. The genetic distinction we are referring to is between those who are fully human and those that carry the genetic trait of the Nephilim. That is the simplicity of what we are discussing. The Anakim, the Emim, and the Zamzummim came through this contaminated genetic line, let alone Goliath and his brothers. Listen to Numbers 13:32, *"All the people we saw there are of great size. ³³ We saw the Nephilim there (the descendants of Anak come from the Nephilim). We seemed like grasshoppers in our own eyes, and we looked the same to them."* I should also mention that many giant skeletal remains have been discovered around the world.

I want to say again that there is controversy about the proper way to interpret this passage, even in the Christian community. The perspective that I learned from one of my teachers at Liberty University was, "When the clear sense makes perfect sense, seek no other sense, or you end up with nonsense." My preference, therefore, is to allow scripture to speak. Not to seek interpretations that might be more comfortable.

Many do not want to believe that this could have occurred. Who would want to believe that demons could procreate and produce offspring with women? However, this does put scripture in a context to answer some of the hard questions in the Bible. We can understand why God would destroy the preflood world. We can understand why he would call Israel to isolate themselves and not intermarry with others. It had nothing to do with ethnicity as we speak of it today. He was keeping the genetic line pure so that the Messiah would come through the line of humanity. We can now understand why God would have them wipe out the entirety of a people when coming into a country. It was to save humanity through the seed of the women ultimately.

We must take into account that God said between your seed and her seed. So, God was not unaware of what was to occur. Some people would interpret this to mean those who follow Satan and those who follow righteousness or those who follow God. But God does personally claim the offspring and say my seed. He says the seed of the women. Remember, at this point, the woman had just fallen into sin. She was now cut off from God and placed in subjection under the authority of the Adversary. So the clear sense would indicate that the passage refers to a child born of her lineage at some time in the future. It could not have been referring to a line of righteousness, especially since we are taught, that there is none righteous, no not one. (Romans 3:10.)

The Flood

In speaking of the flood, it is hard not to notice that almost every culture on the planet has an account of their own about a deluge event. Many are more familiar with the Christian account that we find in the Bible, but other accounts also exist. In ancient Mesopotamia, they have the Epic of Gilgamesh, and it bears remarkable similarities in some areas to our Noahic history. However, it refers to raining down loaves of bread and wheat, later spoken of as water. In Hindu traditions, Manu had acted kindly toward a fish. He was told by a fish he had been kind to that all of humanity was going to be destroyed by a flood. He was directed to build a boat which the fish pulled through the water. The boat landed safely on a mountain top. In the Aztec culture, the man, Coxcox, and his wife were told that the Gods were angry with them and were going to destroy the world with a flood. Being warned of a flood, they hollowed out a log. In Greek Mythology, Deucalion and his wife, Pyrrha, were told Zeus would destroy the world through flood and to build an ark. The ark rested on top of a mountain. To repopulate the earth, they each threw a stone over their shoulders. Those thrown over his became men. The rocks thrown over her shoulders became women. Some wicked tradesmen built a boat and sailed to an island full of spirits in the Buddhist traditions. The spirits became angered at the men, and they were told they would bring a flood over the island. One spirit told them to build a boat, while another spirit told them not to worry. It was not going to happen. One foolish man agreed to party and lived without the worry of the flood, while a wise man built the boat. Those who believed the wise man survived, and those who believed the foolish man did not. There are a few accounts in China; one has a couple who was warned of the flood getting into a gourd to survive the flood. Another tells of a man named Nuah, a righteous man. God warned him of a flood that was coming to destroy mankind because of their wickedness. Nuah built a boat, and he, his wife, three sons, and three daughters were saved.

In Norse legend, the god Ymir turned evil. Villi, Ve, and Odin killed him. His blood spilled out, creating a flood that destroyed almost all of the Jotun. Only two survived by building an ark. Many other cultures talk about a great flood tradition. These traditions have been carried down through generations with incredible similarities to the biblical record: the Aborigines, the Hawaiians, and others. The accounts are not written in the specific details of the Genesis account. Still, they validate the reality of the flood occurring and, from my perspective, verify the reality and the accuracy of the word of God.

Many correlations can be drawn to some of these accounts with the stories of Gods and them getting into arguments and having conflicts. When understood in context, they would fit well with the accounts in the Bible of the Nephilim and the chaos that existed in the days prior to our Genesis flood account. I love that this proves out the truth of the Word of God. The biblical description and the details provided give us the clearest picture of what happened. A flood did occur.

Some archaeologists make the mistake of believing the story in Christianity was taken from these different cultures and adapted for the other mythological, cosmological or theological use. They do this because they too easily dismiss the historical records that are contained in the Bible. Yet, these historical records have been used to find ancient cities that were once thought to be a myth. Once again, proving the veracity of the word of God.

Let me suggest a perspective that makes the most sense. Noah came through the flood with his family. It was from this first post-flood family that the earth was repopulated. Remember that the mDNA goes back to the time of the flood and the three branches that occurred. It is no wonder there are similarities. It might also explain today, the rumors that are going about of non-human DNA strains in the human genome. It is not hard to understand that this knowledge was passed down through the generations into the different extended family locations. Over the years, some of the actual accounts became stories of exaggeration and myth.

An example of this would be passing on ancient knowledge. Could you imagine living over nine hundred years and the knowledge you would accumulate? Let alone God did not create Adam short on intellect. Adam was the one responsible for naming everything. We are told in Genesis 2:19,

> "Out of the ground, the LORD God formed every beast of the field and every bird of the [a]sky, and brought *them* to the man to see what he would call them; and whatever the man called a living creature, that was its name. [20] The man gave names to all the cattle, and to the birds of the [a]sky, and to every beast of the field."

We know the line of Cain developed knowledge of music and forging. There is no difficulty understanding that their knowledge could exceed our own in many ways. Let alone the intellect of the Nephilim having great knowledge. Some of this pre-flood knowledge, which scientists and archaeologists believe we cannot duplicate today, carried over post-flood. Other knowledge did not. Imagine half man and half angelic giants with increased knowledge or possessing great strength. They certainly might be able to move huge stones to build enormous structures. This is, of course, speculation on my part as I seek to understand the big picture.

After the flood, as the first family spread out, various cultures would naturally have similarities, such as pyramid structures, which would be no surprise since the accounts of these things were carried over from Noah and his family.

According to the Bible and several other accounts, we know that the Ark rested on the highest mountain. Chances are, in the post-flood world Noah and his family moved down from the mountain to settle. It is not hard to imagine that in retelling the history of the flood and the Ark resting high in the mountain, it began to take on the idea that the boat came down from the sky, to have landed in the mountains.

Some archaeologists would claim that these other writings came first. There is no evidence the accounts came first. Even if the writings pre-existed the written account of Moses, it does not mean that the accounts pre-existed the history about which Moses wrote. But again, the overlap of knowledge from Adam to Noah and Noah to Abraham is not hard to understand. The maintenance of the actual history that took place should have been able to stay intact.

So why do I mention all of this in relation to the flood and other cultures? I mention it to share the reality of another area of authority, and that is the authority of the Word of God. It is important for us to recognize the distinction between myths that were passed down and a historical account that has been recorded. One has only to read these various accounts to see the Bible's precedence. The Bible demonstrates its authority in revealing these historical accounts.

What is important to understand is that once again, we can see the sovereign authority of God in his ability to judge sin, either on a physical, global, or spiritual level. We know that some fallen angels committed an act more atrocious, and it demanded a greater punishment. They have been locked away until the day of judgment., I am saying that this judgment was due to the acts committed in Genesis 6. As we discussed, the book of Enoch mentions this judgment as well.

God is sovereign. He is also righteous and holy. Satan won legal authority over this world, and God cannot circumvent the authority of the adversary to accomplish His own will. He must work within the boundaries of authority to accomplish His will.

Yet, God laid His plans for the redemption of mankind before the foundation of the world. He called on Noah and used him to save the remanent of mankind. He called on Abraham to keep a line of genetically pure humanity through whom the Messiah could come. This is part of the reason why so many have sought to wipe out the nation of Israel, generation after generation.

Let me be clear about what I am not saying. I am not saying that today Israel is the only pure form of the original seed of the woman.

I am saying that from a biblical perspective, it no longer matters. I do not believe the enemy completely understands this truth. If the Lord locked away the angels who committed such acts and put a stop to this occurring again, then the chances are that the genetic line of Satan has been reduced to something minuscule anyway. At least until now, but that is another story.

The Messiah, Jesus, has already come into the World. He is the seed of the woman promised by God in Genesis who would defeat the serpent of old. We are not saved as a result of genetics anyway. We are saved by faith. Ephesians 2:8-9 reads, "For by grace you have been saved through faith; and that not of yourselves, *it is* the gift of God." Jesus has grafted in those who were not the children of Abraham to make one bride. Remember, the promise to save mankind was given in the garden long before Abraham was born. God has always been the God of the entire universe, not just Israel. It does not matter who you are. The Savior was born of the seed of the woman through the lineage of the people of Israel, but the promise of the Savior is for all. Likewise, the truth is that Israel rejected the Messiah during the time of Jesus, and their rejection resulted in the salvation of the Gentiles. Read this passage carefully. It is very powerful for our understanding. It is Romans 11:11-31.

> [11] I say then, they did not stumble so as to fall, did they? May it never be! But by their transgression salvation has come to the Gentiles, to make them jealous. [12] Now if their transgression is riches for the world and their failure is riches for the Gentiles, how much more will their fulfillment be! [13] But I am speaking to you who are Gentiles. Inasmuch then as I am an apostle of Gentiles, I magnify my ministry, [14] if somehow, I might move to jealousy my fellow countrymen and save some of them. [15] For if their rejection is the reconciliation of the world, what will their acceptance be but life from the dead? [16]

If the first piece of dough is holy, the lump is also; and if the root is holy, the branches are too."

"[17] But if some of the branches were broken off, and you, being a wild olive, were grafted in among them and became partaker with them of the rich root of the olive tree, [18] do not be arrogant toward the branches; but if you are arrogant, remember that it is not you who supports the root, but the root supports you. [19] You will say then, "Branches were broken off so that I might be grafted in." [20] Quite right, they were broken off <u>for their unbelief</u>, but you stand by your faith. Do not be conceited, but fear; [21] for if God did not spare the natural branches, He would not spare you, either. [22] Behold then the kindness and severity of God; to those who fell, severity, but to you, God's kindness, if you continue in His kindness; otherwise, you also will be cut off. [23] And they also, if they do not continue in their unbelief, will be grafted in, for God is able to graft them in again. [24] For if you were cut off from what is by nature a wild olive tree, and were grafted contrary to nature into a cultivated olive tree, how much more will these who are the natural branches be grafted into their own olive tree?"

""[25] For I do not want you, brethren, to be uninformed of this mystery—so that you will not be wise in your own estimation—that a partial hardening has happened to Israel until the fullness of the Gentiles has come in; [26] and so all Israel will be saved; just as it is written,

> "THE DELIVERER WILL COME FROM ZION,
> HE WILL REMOVE UNGODLINESS FROM JACOB."

> ²⁷ "This is My covenant with them,
> when I take away their sins."
>
> "²⁸ From the standpoint of the gospel, they are enemies for your sake, but from the standpoint of God's choice they are beloved for the sake of the fathers; ²⁹ for the gifts and the calling of God are irrevocable. ³⁰ For just as you once were disobedient to God, but now have been shown mercy because of their disobedience, ³¹ so these also now have been disobedient, that because of the mercy shown to you they also may now be shown mercy."

There is certainly a lot to unpack there, and I will not hit on it all, but I do want to point out that Israel became arrogant in their own standing, and it is likewise the tendency of the Christian church today to do the same. This arrogance is certainly one of the reasons we have so much conflict in the Christian church. We must remain humble, as we are these branches who have been grafted in knowing that this is the plan of God, and that the rejection of the Messiah by Israel resulted in our salvation.

Second is the fact that the promises of God are not based on lineage. They are based on faith. We can clearly see this in the passage. Those of Israel who were cut off, were cut off because of <u>unbelief.</u> In their own arrogance as the children of God, they relied more on their heritage than their faith. Yet, the promises of God to Abraham came to him by faith. As you may know, Abraham was in the line of Shem, and it would follow therefore, that he was genetically pure. Salvation has always come as a result of faith. It is faith that results in obedience. Faith moves us to take action. This was how it was with Noah, and this is how it was with Abraham. It is also the way it is with us too.

I know this is a lot to take in, especially if you consider that this may mean that many of us are not genetically pure in line with the

THE SPIRITUAL REALM

original creation of man. Therein lies the most difficulty with this perspective. In truth, we have not been as God designed us since the fall anyway. God created us to be alive spiritually, and as a result of sin, we were dead. God created us to walk in the garden with Him and live directly in this relationship with Him. But that has not occurred since the fall either. We might think that all has been restored through the victory won by Jesus, but that is not the truth. We still live in a fallen world that is held in the bondage of spiritual darkness through the power of sin, and we still live in a human body marred from the fall and prone to sin. The reality is that our flesh is marred and condemned and will not be saved. That is why we will receive a new body. Read this passage from Romans 7:14-25,

> "*^{14} For we know that the Law is spiritual, but I am of flesh, sold into bondage to sin. ^{15} For what I am doing, I do not understand; for I am not practicing what I would like to do, but I am doing the very thing I hate. ^{16} But if I do the very thing I do not want to do, I agree with the Law, confessing that the Law is good. ^{17} So now, no longer am I the one doing it, but sin which dwells in me. ^{18} For I know that nothing good dwells in me, that is, in my flesh; for the willing is present in me, but the doing of the good is not. ^{19} For the good that I want, I do not do, but I practice the very evil that I do not want. ^{20} But if I am doing the very thing I do not want, I am no longer the one doing it, but sin which dwells in me.*
>
> *^{21} I find then the principle that evil is present in me, the one who wants to do good. ^{22} For I joyfully concur with the law of God in the inner man, ^{23} but I see a different law in the members of my body, waging war against the law of my mind and making me a prisoner of the law of sin which is in my members. ^{24} Wretched man*

> that I am! Who will set me free from the body of this death? ²⁵ Thanks be to God through Jesus Christ our Lord! So then, on the one hand I myself with my mind am serving the law of God, but on the other, with my flesh the law of sin."

When you read the Romans 11:11-31 passage of scripture with this truth in mind, you will start to understand things that may previously have not made sense. But scripture teaches us that those who were outside the nation of Israel have been grafted in. All who come to faith in Jesus are made joint heirs with Jesus. We are taught in this passage from Romans 11:11-31 that the key to being grafted in is belief.

The great reality today is the issue of faith. When we place our faith in the Messiah, the savior, sent by God to make that payment for sin that you and I owe, it results in being made alive again in the spirit. Once again, we are removed from under the authority of Satan and brought under the authority of Jesus. The only actual distinction that exists today is the one between those who are alive in the spirit and those who are not. Romans 8:16-17 reads, " The Spirit Himself testifies with our spirit that we are children of God, ¹⁷ and if children, heirs also, heirs of God and fellow heirs with Christ."

Future Fulfillment:

Something else we need to take a moment to discuss is the future fulfillment of the seed of the woman defeating the seed of the adversary, Satan. This is something we have not seen. Most often, people consider the victory of Christ at the cross fulfilling this prophetic statement from Genesis, but that is not the case. I want us to realize that in the same way there was a literal biological child from the woman's line, there will also be a literal physical child in the line of the adversary. The seed of the woman still must "bruise him on the head". This can be applied spiritually to the victory of Jesus on the cross, defeating

Satan for the spiritual restoration of those who believe, but we have not dealt yet with the physical world.

Genesis 3:15,

> "And I will put enmity between you and the woman,
> And between your seed and her Seed; He shall bruise you on the head, And you shall bruise Him on the heel.

This event has not yet occurred. When Jesus defeated Satan, it was a spiritual victory providing life everlasting to those who would come to repentance and receive forgiveness through faith in the completed work of Jesus. In one sense, Satan did not have his head crushed, the head is where the crown of a king sits. It is the demonstration of authority. Jesus crushed the authority of Satan from a spiritual perspective, but Satan is still in authority over this world. Jesus has not taken possession yet. Therefore, this event could not be referring to Calvary, so what are we talking about? I believe it is referring to the coming victory of Jesus over the anti-Christ. It is prophetically culminating in the Valley of Jezreel, the battle of Armageddon. That will be the actual time of fulfillment for the Genesis 3:15 prophecy. The victory over the kingdom of darkness has already been won through Jesus' completed work on the cross. That is, sin no longer has the power to hold a person in the bondage of sin and the kingdom of darkness. They can be free, forgiven, and brought into kinship with Jesus. The person can be set free from the kingdom of darkness while the enemy retains control of that kingdom. But this man of lawlessness has yet to be dealt with. I am not sure why we in the Christian community often point to the cross as the only fulfillment when we understand that this other battle is to come in Bible prophecy when the anti-Christ has risen to power. For this to occur, there will probably be another violation of God's boundaries, and the abomination that occurred before resulting in the Nephilim will occur at least one time more. Since it is the seed of the adversary, Satan, whom the seed of the woman will crush, then the anti-Christ will be genetically compromised lineage of the adversary.

I find it interesting that this whole agenda is coming into play with all the mutant and mutation propaganda from Hollywood and in the realm of science, promoting the genetic modification of humanity through such instruments as vaccines. This week, November 2021, we saw a report from the Director of National intelligence, Avril Haines, comment on the possibility of extraterrestrial or even extra-dimensional life. From my perspective, I look to overt demonic appearances seeking to prepare the way for the antichrist. At this time, I firmly believe this "man of lawlessness" (2 Thessalonians 2:1-12) is already in power on the planet and will soon be, if not already, revealed on the world stage.

We must understand that Satan has set his mind against all things Godly. He has made himself an enemy of God. He seeks the destruction of God and the destruction of the knowledge of God. Likewise, he seeks the destruction of those who belong to God and the destruction of the order that God created in everything. He seeks to pervert the truth and to keep as many as possible trapped in sin and under his authority.

Today, we continually witness laws passed in our country by many of our political leaders that are directly in opposition to the clear teaching of scriptures. In a very real sense, they make our world today worse than in the days of Noah. The same type of corruption is occurring in our societies, but we go even further and pass laws to protect it. We can even witness those who say they are believers defending such practices. We call these believers apostate, meaning they have fallen away from sound teaching. They chose to believe the world over the word. There is a wonderful truth for us to understand in all of this. The Messiah, who has come victoriously as a meek and humble Lamb, will return as a victorious lion. Revelation 5:5 reads, "Behold, the Lion of the tribe of Judah, the Root of David, has prevailed to open the scroll and to loose its seven seals"

Chapter 10

AUTHORITY OF FOLLOWERS OF JESUS

Two Kingdoms

It would be easy to misunderstand that the distinction between the two kingdoms is one of the physical realm, and the other the spiritual realm, but this is not the case. While both the physical and spiritual realms exist, the kingdoms are not divided by that distinction. It is more the distinction of citizenship then type. We have already come to understand that there is a kingdom of darkness. The kingdom of darkness includes not just the fallen physical world. It includes those who are fallen that dwell in the spiritual world too. Today's distinction is that of the kingdom of darkness and the kingdom of light. As we have seen, according to scripture, if you have entered into a relationship with Jesus, you are part of the kingdom of light. We are taught in John 1:7-8,

> *"1 In the beginning was the Word, and the Word was with God, and the Word was God. ²He was in the beginning with God. ³ All things came into being through Him, and apart from Him nothing came into being that has come into being. ⁴ In Him was life, and the life was the*

> Light of men. *⁵ The Light shines in the darkness, and the darkness did not comprehend it.*
>
> *⁶ There came a man sent from God, whose name was John. ⁷He came as a witness, to testify about the Light, so that all might believe through him. ⁸ He was not the Light, but he came to testify about the Light."*

Jesus is the light of the world. Again Colossians 1:27 "to whom God willed to make known what is the riches of the glory of this mystery among the Gentiles, which is Christ in you, the hope of glory."

In speaking to the disciples, Jesus said to them in Matthew 5:14-16, "You are the light of the world. A town built on a hill cannot be hidden. ¹⁵ Neither do people light a lamp and put it under a bowl. Instead, they put it on its stand, and it gives light to everyone in the house. ¹⁶ In the same way, let your light shine before others, that they may see your good deeds and glorify your Father in heaven." And again from 1 John 4:4, "You, dear children, are from God and have overcome them, because the one who is in you is greater than the one who is in the world."

The Holy Spirit is the basis of that rekindled life that we have through Christ. The Holy Spirit is given as a helper and as a promise. Ephesians 4:30 tells us, "Do not grieve the Holy Spirit of God, by whom you were sealed for the day of redemption." The light of life found in Jesus exists in every believer. We are not citizens of the kingdoms of the world, which are in darkness. We are citizens of the kingdom of light. The difficulty is that as citizens of the kingdom of light, we currently dwell within the kingdom of darkness. We are in the domain of our enemy. The more we seek to live as children of the kingdom of light while dwelling in the realm of darkness, the more the enemy of God and his minions will take notice.

When I was in the infantry, we were taught about not smoking on night watch because an enemy out there somewhere in the darkness can see the light of your match a long way off. It immediately grabs their attention. The old story warned that you should not be the third person in the match because they would notice the first person, seek to acquire the target on the second, and adjust and fire on the third. If you are a believer in the Lord Jesus, you are an enemy of the enemy of God. Likewise, as we dwell in the kingdom of darkness, the light of life in Jesus that we possess stands out in contrast to the surrounding darkness. To those living in darkness, we should look peculiar. We should look different to them. They should recognize that we are not the same.

One of my first mentors that God brought into my life was a guy named Roger Donald. He was an ex-hockey player out of Canada. He came to Christ and became a writer and lyricist for different artists like Lisa Whelchel, and Joe English, the former drummer for Paul McCartney and Wings. Roger was amazing to me in that he was the first person to help me grow in my faith as a believer in Jesus. I remember he would always ask me, "What are you doing?" I would answer, and he would say to me, "Why are you doing that?" I would give some excuse, and he would say, "Yes, but God's word says this." Roger was willing to hold me accountable for my behavior. It was at that time that something in me changed. Even though I was dwelling in the kingdom of darkness, I started living in the kingdom of light. I noticed that God was at work in my heart. I started seeing a change within me. Rather than feeling I had to put things in my life aside as a Christian, I wanted to put them aside. In the beginning, I felt I had to surrender my will to do his will. Then it came to the point where it was my will to do his will. My joy was in pleasing God. It was at this point I started to understand the difference between the kingdom of darkness and the kingdom of light.

However, all of that backstory to say that Roger once told me that I could be sitting on a barstool and the guy to the right of me might start pouring his life out to me, and the person to my left might be angry and aggressive toward me. Neither of them knew me from anyone.

The point being is that it was not me they were reacting to, but the Holy Spirit within me. If you are a believer then God is at work in you.

I saw the truth that Roger talked about while I was in the Navy. I had just reported aboard my ship, and I was walking down the passageway toward my berthing area. As I walked past a couple talking in the passageway, they started swearing at me. I literally did not know anyone on this ship. I found out later that this couple proclaimed themselves to be Satanists. It was not me they were responding to but the Holy Spirit within me, just as Roger had stated.

When you become a believer in the Lord Jesus, a real and literal change takes place. You are no longer the person you once were. Your citizenship has been transferred from the kingdom of darkness to the Kingdom of Light by faith. This light is life in Christ Jesus our Lord, and you have been sealed with the Holy Spirit of God.

We have already talked about the spiritual realm and how there may exist around us right now many entities in the spiritual realm. Possibly, both ministering angels as well as demons. I am not saying that they are around you right now at this moment, but I do believe they could be. Some would explain it as another dimension. Maybe that is the best way to describe it. Another would be that they are spiritual forces at work in the physical realm. They can see us and exactly what we are doing, and we cannot see them. I believe that we can clearly sense them many times in our lives. But again, people are wired differently. It is kind of like trying to tune in to an old radio. Sometimes the reception is better than others.

The Bible in 1 Peter 2:9, tells us that we, as believers, have been taken out of the kingdom of darkness and brought into his marvelous light. Colossians 1:13 reads, "For He rescued us from the domain of darkness and transferred us to the kingdom of His beloved Son." You can begin to understand that the difference between these two kingdoms is one of authority. If we are servants of Jesus, then we obey Jesus. Sometimes hearing the guiding and directing of God is difficult. His voice can be hard to hear because we currently abide in the

Kingdom of darkness. Listen to Romans 6:16, "Do you not know that when you present yourselves to someone *as* slaves for obedience, you are slaves of the one whom you obey, either of sin resulting in death, or of obedience resulting in righteousness?" It is difficult for the children of light who have identified with the darkness for so long. We naturally, through our flesh, relate to the darkness. Our flesh is accustomed to operating in this realm by chasing after its own desires. As children of the light, we have to submit ourselves under the Lordship of the author of the light. That is Jesus. Likewise, we must learn to walk in the counsel of the Holy Spirit.

We have to learn to understand what it means to walk in the light. This is discipleship. As we become more experienced at following the Lord and walking in the light, we will begin to experience victory over the darkness. But we must know that the darkness is relentless, and every time we falter, the darkness crowds in on us. 1 John 1:7 teaches us, "but if we walk in the Light as He Himself is in the Light, we have fellowship with one another, and the blood of Jesus His Son cleanses us from all sin." To walk in the light is to walk in the Spirit of God who indwells us. We talked about this previously. As our flesh relates to the world around us, so the spirit is our connection with God. There is so much in scripture about this very truth. Galatians 5:16 reads, "But I say, walk by the Spirit, and you will not carry out the desire of the flesh." Romans 5:5-8,

> "Those who live according to the flesh set their minds on the things of the flesh; but those who live according to the Spirit set their minds on the things of the Spirit. The mind of the flesh is death, but the mind of the Spirit is life and peace, because the mind of the flesh is hostile to God: It does not submit to God's law, nor can it do so. Those controlled by the flesh cannot please God."

I have said for years that it is simple, if you die under Satan's authority, you will have Satan's eternity. If you die under the authority of Jesus, you will have the same eternity as Jesus. We have seen in Romans 8:17, "and if children, heirs also, heirs of God and fellow heirs with Christ."

While this is good news for us who know Jesus, this is not good news for those still in the bondage of sin. We need to recognize that from this two-kingdom perspective, we are ambassadors for Christ. 2 Corinthians 5:20-21 reads,

> "Therefore, we are ambassadors for Christ, as though God were making an appeal through us; we beg you on behalf of Christ, be reconciled to God. He made Him who knew no sin *to be* sin on our behalf, so that we might become the righteousness of God in Him."

We are here for a reason. We have a purpose. We represent a God who is loving and who is kind. He wants to see everyone saved. It is not his desire that anyone should be lost to the kingdom of darkness. Listen to this verse in 2 Peter 3:9, "⁹ The Lord is not slow about His promise, as some count slowness, but is patient toward you, not wishing for any to perish but for ALL to come to repentance." It is not the will of God that anyone should spend eternity suffering a fate that was meant for Satan and demons. Matthew 25:41, ""Then He will also say to those on His left, 'Depart from Me, you accursed people, into the eternal fire which has been prepared for the devil and his angels." It is His will that all would come into His kingdom and spend an eternity with Him. That choice, however, He leaves for each of us to make.

I met my wife when I was in the military stationed in Scotland. We were married in Scotland, and then a few years later, I was transferred to Miramar, the old Top Gun school in California. After about twenty years of marriage and living in the United States, my wife decided to become an American citizen. She went through the process required by the government to become a citizen of this country. She raised her hand and took the oath. It was completely her choice to make. I never once asked her or coerced her to become a citizen of our great nation. It is the same for the kingdom of God. It is completely voluntary. God will not force you to become a citizen of the kingdom of light. A person is free to remain in the kingdom of darkness if that is their decision. Likewise, it is not something that happens by accident. It is an intentional act on your part.

I had a season in my life when I would spend my paychecks on gospel tracts, and at every opportunity, I would take a taxi to the ferry, a ferry to the train, and a train into the city. I would hand out these simple messages to anyone I could. I would try and get into conversations with them and tell them about the love of Jesus for them. I was not out there for me. It had nothing to do with me. I simply recognized that I have literally never locked eyes with a person that Jesus does not love and did not die for. They mattered to Him, so they mattered to me.

We may remain physically in the kingdom of darkness, but we are free. As believers, it has to be our goal to see those in the bondage of sin held to the kingdom of darkness come into the light. There is a saying that comes from Colossians 1:27 that I have shared already, it reads, "to whom God willed to make known what is the riches of the glory of this mystery among the Gentiles, which is Christ in you, the hope of glory." and from 1 Corinthians 2:6-8, "Which none of the rulers of this age has understood; for if they had understood it they would not have crucified the Lord of glory." Instead of having only one Jesus to deal with Satan, now has to deal with Jesus indwelling each and every believer. So instead of one Jesus, there is an army of believers seeking to serve and honor God faithfully. Instead of a light, we should be a raging bonfire. Our light reaches deeper into the darkness.

The Church

I want to share a perspective with you. It is the idea that today, for the most part, the "Christian church" has it wrong. I am NOT saying that the Christian church is bad and that we should turn out back on it? Of course not. What I mean is this. For the most part, we Christians have forgotten that we are the church, the body of Christ. We have adopted the idea that church is something we go to, not something we are. This has led to the church becoming an institution. For the most part, we abdicated religious instruction to the church and the professional and volunteer staff at the church. I have even heard pastors teach their congregations from the pulpit that going to church is a relevant mark of their Christian faith. It becomes one of the boxes we check off to feel good about ourselves and our Christian walk. Being the church is not the same thing as going to church.

As believers, we are to study scriptures ourselves as taught in 2 Timothy 2:15, "Study to shew thyself approved unto God, a workman that needing not to be ashamed, rightly dividing the word of truth." Likewise, we should act as the Bereans did in Acts 17:11, "Now these people were more noble-minded than those in Thessalonica, for they received the word with great eagerness, examining the Scriptures daily *to see* whether these things were so." Today, we essentially rely on others to study for us and tell us what the Bible teaches. We simply attend church to mark off the little box confirming we are believers and we have fulfilled our obligation by attending. I call it our good Christian checklist. Even our primary method of evangelism is to invite friends to church so that someone can tell them about Jesus.

A church itself may grow in numbers, but that does not mean it has grown in depth. Nor that God is blessing it. Often, when a church grows, it begins to cater to the perceived needs of those attending the church. The goal is that they will have their spiritual needs and the needs of their families met. That is a noble goal. But it drives a consumer mentality, and if the church fails in meeting their perceived needs, the people go and seek out a church they feel will meet those needs. The problem is that they have lost focus. The focal point of ministry has become the people rather than the God the people are supposed to worship and serve. The result has been that many churches seek to become more like the world around them. They do this in an effort to keep the numbers up in the church and, of course, the tithing since all of the developed programs demand a cost. In the presentation of worship and the word of God, they entertain so that unbelievers will enjoy themselves and come back. We put together program after program, and hopefully, we will be able to, at some point, reach them with the good news of Jesus.

I was applying for an associate position at a church in southern California back in the mid-nineties. The senior pastor recommended that we attend a service first to see what we thought. I became physically nauseous at the service. I won't go into detail, but I will say it was not focused on the Word of God or even preaching the Word of God. I asked the pastor when we met afterward the service when they shared the good news of Jesus. He said he thought they occasionally did on Wednesdays.

I have often heard the church referred to as a hospital where the sick can come for help. I want to say a few things about this perspective. One, if they come to the church because they recognize they are sick, we need to provide the cure. The cure is Jesus. Jesus is the only cure for their disease, sin. The church should never seek to be a substitute for Jesus. Likewise, if we are not being clear about sharing who Jesus is and what He has done for humanity, then that analogy would be making them sit in the hospital's foyer until you feel they are sincerely ready for the doctor. Second is the idea that the role of the Christian is to invite people to the hospital. Why would you go to a hospital when you do not realize you are sick? I would put forth to you that the Christian should be more like a paramedic going out to meet those afflicted and provide the assistance that is needed. This analogy meets the "Go ye therefore" instruction provided by Jesus in Matthew 28:19-20. As paramedics go out in two (pair of medics, sorry dad joke), Jesus sent out the disciples in groups of two. Paramedics also receive training prior to going out to minister to the community's medical needs. Likewise, we must train people to accomplish the mission of the church. Every aspect of the church should be mission minded. While every church may have its unique personality, every church is called and united in the same mission. It is not to grow the church bigger. It is to grow the kingdom bigger by rescuing those still trapped in the bondage of sin. Those of the Light must seek to reach those still in darkness.

If you have not yet caught on, the church's role is to worship and praise the God who has saved us. The focus of this worship is always on the Lord. When we come to church, we should always surrender and be humble before our loving God. The purpose is also to train for the mission Jesus has called the church to perform. We train and send forth. Certainly, there are churches that still take this approach, but I have to tell you that the majority do not. They are inward-focused rather than outreach-focused. One of the most attended classes I have taught in the local church has been on evangelism. The classes are always well attended until the day comes, we are going into the community to practice what we have learned, then hardly anyone shows. Other pastors have told me that they have had this same experience.

We were never called to stay indoors and appease ourselves by sending checks to support distant missionaries. One of my favorite passages is when Jesus, in his parting words makes the statement found in Matthew 28:18-20,

> "And Jesus came up and spoke to them, saying, "All authority has been given to Me in heaven and on earth. [19] [a]Go therefore and make disciples of all the nations, baptizing them in the name of the Father and the Son and the Holy Spirit, [20] teaching them to observe all that I commanded you; and lo, I am with you [b]always, even to the end of the age."

I want us to first recognize that Jesus has authority. Authority is the guiding theme of the Bible. Here we have Jesus proclaiming his victory over Satan and the reclamation of authority. So, what does He say? ALL authority has been given to me. In other words, He is saying. I have the authority to tell you to go and do what I am about to tell you to go and do! In this case, to GO! We are to go forth. We are to go out. We are to do the same thing that Jesus had taught the disciples to do: go into the communities and reach those still in darkness with the message of truth.

The church is more than just a single match that an enemy may notice in the night. We can light a single match, but these matches coming together should be impossible not to notice. The church should be more like lighting a brush fire.

I remember when we were kids. My parents took us to California to visit my maternal grandparents. Their property was in the hills of California. My two brothers and I were in one of the fields not too far from the house, and one off my brothers was a smoker and my other brother was lighting the cigarette for him. He struck the match and lit the cigarette and shaking the match out threw it to the ground. As it happened, the matches did not go out, and as it hit the dry grass, the grass went up in flames. There was a horse trough nearby, and we were trying to get water and run it over to douse the fire, but it was spreading too fast. Then the fire hit the hill, and it took off. There was no stopping it. Forty acres later, with the help of planes and fire engines, the fire was out. That is a great picture of the church! That is what we are to be. The only difference is instead of bringing destruction, we bring light and life into the kingdom of darkness. Interesting that when a fire is that big, you can even see the evidence of it during the day when you have acre after acre burning! That is our goal and our mission. We go into all the world.

Can you imagine the impact of the Christian church, the body of Christ, on the world around us if our goal in coming together was to surrender our hearts in obedience through worship and equip the body of Christ to go forth to accomplish our missional mandate? When we operate in this way, the enemy takes notice, and the attacks from this enemy multiply. He does not care about inwardly focused, ineffective churches unless you are starting to wake up. When you do, he will take notice, and the spiritual attacks will happen. These attacks will even come from within the body of the church.

When I became a pastor, I had already experienced the reality of spiritual warfare. I did not expect that the enemy would attack from within the church, especially from those who were supposed to be leaders. The attacks from within the church are the hardest to combat because they are from people you have come to love and serve within the body of Christ. I say this to encourage you to love and support your pastors. They are under spiritual attack at a different level than most others, and they need your prayer and support.

The body of Christ must have the attitude of surrender to the Lord. This humble attitude is what worship is all about. Jesus is the Lord, not us. We submit our will under his authority. Also, churches must have an attitude of surrender to the Word of God for the equipping of the body to fulfill the church's mission. What I am talking about here is submission to the authority of the Lord and to the Word of God, the Bible. The believer is under the authority of both. Notice I did not say to the church. Although if a pastor and a church are following scriptures, it should be easy to come under the authority of pastoral leadership in your church. I do believe in pastoral servant/ leadership. But if you are not in a church preaching sound doctrine and hold fast to the Bible, then flee from there and find a Bible-believing, Bible-preaching church.

I am of the belief that members of a church should be taught what to expect about faithfully working to fulfill their mission. We have been called to a purpose. Just as with that brush fire when we were kids, the enemy will break out the planes and fire engines, and he will try to stop the church from reaching the lost in the kingdom of darkness. He will use his tools of division, diversion, and distraction to destroy the work and the people until there exist only smoldering remains of an ineffective church. We have to understand that a church of the Word is different from a church of the World.

I have said for decades that there is a chasm being drawn wide and wider between those who say they are believers and those who are believers. Between those who say they are part of the church and those who are the church. When the church becomes an institution, it is easy for the enemy to infiltrate and destroy any meaningful progress. The great news is that today people are awakening to this reality. The church is coming alive with its purpose and with a renewed understanding of its mission.

I want to state again that I am not saying the church has become a horrible place that should be avoided. I AM saying that it is easy to lose focus on the actual purpose of ministry. We are all imperfect and fallible. It is easy for people take possession of something that belongs only to God. We must always recognize the church is his. Our goal as believers is to remain faithful to what HE has called us to do. The first purpose of church leadership is always to ensure the church remains in the hands of the Lord. Likewise, the focus of ministry always remains the mission that He has called us to accomplish. Everything else comes after.

Regarding the church, I want to state again that it is not our church. It is his church. It belongs to Jesus. We must always be aware that people will seek to take possession of the church. Even well-intentioned people. When I was pastoring a small church, I remember once, I heard a board member get upset and make the statement, "Pastors come and go, but this is MY church." You can see that he has taken possession of something that, in reality, does not belong to him. It only belongs to Jesus. Jesus stated in Matthew 16:18, "I also say to you that you are Peter, and upon this rock, I will build My church; and the gates of Hell shall not prevail against it." It is his church, not ours. In the same way, we are his He is not ours. He has the authority, not us. Jesus has given us authority for the purpose of accomplishing his mission, but Christ is the head of the church. Our responsibility is to be faithful.

Holy Spirit

The Holy Spirit is a hard concept for many to understand. Certainly, this area of theology has caused much controversy and even great division in the Christian church. I have seen theological positions go to extremes in either direction. I do not seek to resolve this controversy here. This book is not designed for that reason. I do want us to understand that the true believer of God is made alive again in the spirit. John talks about this in John 6:63 when he says, "It is the Spirit who gives life." Probably more familiar is John 3:1-8,

> "Now there was a man of the Pharisees, named Nicodemus, a ruler of the Jews; this man came to Jesus by night and said to Him, "Rabbi, we know that You have come from God *as* a teacher; for no one can do these signs that You do unless God is with him." Jesus answered and said to him, "Truly, truly, I say to you, unless one is born again, he cannot see the kingdom of God."

> "[4] Nicodemus said to Him, "How can a man be born when he is old? He cannot enter a second time into his mother's womb and be born, can he?" Jesus answered, "Truly, truly, I say to you, unless one is born of water and the Spirit he cannot enter into the kingdom of God. That which is born of the flesh is flesh, and that which is born of the Spirit is spirit. Do not be amazed that I said to you, 'You must be born again.' The wind blows where it wishes and you hear the sound of it, but do

not know where it comes from and where it is going; so is everyone who is born of the Spirit."

Some of the cults will take this passage out of context and say that a person must be baptized since it mentions that you must be born of water and spirit, but the conversation here is not about baptism. In this passage, Jesus is telling him that we are born once in the flesh. We come through the water of the womb. The embryotic fluid. We must also be born of the spirit. When he is talking about the flesh, he refers to the natural context of the passage to our physical birth into this world. The second birth is in the spirit. We must be born two times. The first birth is physical; the second birth is spiritual. He actually explains this in the above passage when He writes, "That which is born of the flesh is flesh, and that which is born of the Spirit is spirit."

We have already discovered that humankind already died in the indwelling of the Holy Spirit of God at the time of the fall. After that time, every person born was born body, soul, and dead in spirit. Through the death of Jesus, we receive forgiveness of sin, and the consequence of sin, spiritual death, is removed. We are made alive again in the spirit. Our spirit is made alive by the joining, reconciling with the spirit of God. We have now been born in the flesh, and the second time in the spirit. This is being born again.

I have preached for many years that we are either born once and die twice or born twice and die once. To explain this statement, If we are born in the flesh only, we will die physically and spiritually being forever cut off from God. If we are born of the flesh and the spirit, we will only die physically in the flesh, since spiritually, we will be alive forever with God.

As it was sin that caused spiritual death when that sin is removed, then sin no longer is an issue. Sin is removed through faith in Jesus, leading to repentance and when we are forgiven, we are made alive in the spirit. Where we were once body, soul, and dead in spirit, we are now body, soul, and alive in the spirit. God created us to have life in the spirit and a relationship with Him. After becoming believers, we must learn to walk in the newness of this life in the spirit.

The major obstacle that gets in the way of our success is when we succumb to what scripture calls the "Old Man Nature" or the old self. Colossians 3:9-10 tells us, "Do not lie to one another, since you laid aside the old self with its *evil* practices and have put on the new self who is being renewed to a true knowledge according to the image of the One who created him."

The big idea is this. We used to live according to the power of the flesh, the old man nature. Now we live according to the newness of life through the spirit of God. Before Jesus, I had no choice. I only knew one way to live, and that was through the flesh. I lived under the authority of the flesh. It reigned supreme as I related to the world around me. I was a victim enslaved in the bondage of sin through the flesh. I knew no other way. I walked as a slave to the kingdom of darkness. I had no knowledge of another way to operate. I lived in the world, and I made choices according to my flesh.

I want to point out here that we may have experienced a sense of morality, and that is good, but it is not the same as being alive in the spirit. There are good people from a moral perspective, who are not saved. Once we are alive in the spirit, we can learn to walk by the power of the spirit. Now, we can live under the authority of the spirit. I can make choices that are directed by spirit and in line with the kingdom of light.

We need to understand that on the one hand, we have obtained the promise of our inheritance through the indwelling of the spirit, and we are under the authority of Jesus and can live according to the power of the spirit rather than the flesh. I want us to see Ephesians 1:13-14, *In Him, you also, after listening to the message of truth, the gospel of your salvation—having also believed, you were sealed in Him with the Holy Spirit of promise, who is given as a pledge of our inheritance."* Every true believer has the indwelling of the Holy Spirit of God. They have been made alive in the spirit. Apart from the spirit, there is no life.

Again, we must understand that while alive in the spirit, we still walk in the darkness of the fallen world that seeks to maintain power over us through the weakness of our flesh.

Covering for sin

In the Old Testament, the nation of Israel had many sacrifices for sin. These sacrifices were a covering for sin. They were not the restorative payment that was promised in Genesis 3:15. If we go by the parable of Lazarus and the rich man found in Luke 16,

> "[19] "Now there was a rich man, and he habitually dressed in purple and fine linen, joyously living in splendor every day. [20] And a poor man named Lazarus was laid at his gate, covered with sores, [21] and longing to be fed with the crumbs which were falling from the rich man's table; besides, even the dogs were coming and licking his sores. [22] Now the poor man died and was carried away by the angels to Abraham's bosom; and the rich man also died and was buried. [23] In Hades he lifted up his eyes, being in torment, and *saw Abraham far away and Lazarus in his bosom. [24] And he cried out and said, 'Father Abraham, have mercy on me, and send Lazarus so that he may dip the tip of his finger in water and cool off my tongue, for I am in agony in this flame.' [25] But Abraham said, 'Child, remember that during your life you received your good things, and likewise Lazarus bad things; but now he is being comforted here, and you are in agony. [26] And besides all this, between us and you there is a great chasm fixed, so that those who wish to come over from here to you will not be able,

> *and that none may cross over from there to us.' ²⁷ And he said, 'Then I beg you, father, that you send him to my father's house— ²⁸ for I have five brothers—in order that he may warn them, so that they will not also come to this place of torment.' ²⁹ But Abraham *said, 'They have Moses and the Prophets; let them hear them.' ³⁰ But he said, 'No, father Abraham, but if someone goes to them from the dead, they will repent!' ³¹ But he said to him, 'If they do not listen to Moses and the Prophets, they will not be persuaded even if someone rises from the dead.'"*

Suppose this parable reveals the truth to us about what occurred after the death of Jesus. In that case, we can begin to understand that when someone died in faith before the sacrifice of Jesus, they went to a place called Abraham's bosom (vs.22), or when Jesus was talking to the thief on the cross before his death, He told him he would be with Him that day in paradise (Luke 23:43). They did not go to the area of torment as did the rich man, called Hades (vs. 23 above). They were in a place where they could find comfort in one another.

The sacrifice of Jesus was something different. He was not a covering for sin but a propitiation for sin (1 John 2:2). Propitiation means two things; satisfying the wrath of the one offended and being reconciled and restored in the relationship. In other words, Jesus was a one hundred percent satisfactory payment for sin. That was the means for restoring our relationship with our creator. There is nothing you could add to it, and there is no necessity to add anything to it. The payment of Jesus was once and for all.

In the parable of the rich man, we discover that hell is referred to as having two sections; hades (vs.23) and Abraham's Bosom (vs.22). Likewise, it is described as having a chasm between the two sections. Those who died with faith in God and the promised Messiah went to Abraham's Bosom, and those who died apart from faith went to Hades.

After Jesus made the payment for our sin, we see something entirely different. The apostle Paul suffered a lot at the hands of those he tried to reach with the message of salvation through Jesus. When he was preaching at a town called Lystra, the Jews who were stirring up trouble against the Christians followed him. We read about this in Acts 14:19, *"But Jews came from Antioch and Iconium, and having persuaded the crowds, they stoned Paul and dragged him out of the city, supposing that he was dead."* Some, including me, believe Paul actually died in this encounter, and God brought him back to life, which is why in 2 Corinthians 5:8, Paul can say, *"I say, and prefer rather to be absent from the body and to be at home with the Lord."* Or in Philippians 1:21, "For to me, ªto live is Christ and to die is gain." I like this contrast between the parable of the rich man and the account of the Apostle Paul because it reveals something distinctly changed as a result of the victory won by Jesus. We can see that after the victory, we are taught that when a person dies with faith in Jesus, they do not go to Abraham's bosom; they go to heaven and exist in the presence of God.

What happened when Jesus died

Now there is, of course, as with everything else, some controversy in the Christian church about where Jesus went when he died. His physical body hung on the cross until it was taken down and moved into the tomb, remaining there until His resurrection. What we are referring to, therefore, is where his spirit went after his physical death on the cross.

One perspective teaches that when Jesus died, He went to heaven and spent three days with the Father before returning to His body which was made new, at the resurrection. They garner this idea from Luke 23:46, which reads, "And Jesus, crying out with a loud voice, said, "Father, INTO YOUR HANDS, I COMMIT MY SPIRIT." Having said this, He breathed His last." They interpret this to mean that as Jesus died, His spirit went to the Father. They link this to the statement of Jesus to the thief on the cross found in Luke 23:43, ". "And He said to him, "Truly I say to you, today you will be with Me in Paradise." I can understand how they may draw this conclusion, but I believe it overlooks other relevant scriptures.

When Jesus said these words in Luke 23:46, "Father, INTO YOUR HANDS I COMMIT MY SPIRIT." I believe He was not stating that He was going to the Father but that He was trusting the Father to see Him through what was to come next. We can see this in passages such as Psalm 37:5, "Commit thy way unto the LORD; trust also in Him; and He shall bring it to pass." His statement of committing His spirit into the hands of the Father were not about the physical pain He was enduring. Remember the words Jesus spoke in Matthew 27:46, "Jesus cried out with a loud voice, saying, "ELI, ELI, LAMA SABACHTHANI?" that is, "MY GOD, MY GOD, WHY HAVE YOU FORSAKEN ME?" These words are also found in Psalm 22:1-5,

> "My God, my God, why have You forsaken me?
> Far from my deliverance are the words of my groaning.
> ² O my God, I cry by day, but You do not answer; And by night, but I have no rest. ³ Yet You are holy, O You who are enthroned upon the praises of Israel. ⁴ In You our fathers trusted; They trusted and You delivered them. ⁵ To You they cried out and were delivered; In You they trusted and were not disappointed."

At least one hundred verses talk about the death of Jesus as an atonement for our sin. All of our sin was poured out upon Him. He was the propitiation for our sin. If we remember that sin brought in the physical degeneration of the body and the "spiritual death" or separation from God, then it would make sense that Jesus would have to atone for both. Rather than just bearing our sins on the cross, which He did, Father poured out his wrath on the Son for the sins of all humanity. All sins, past, present, and future would be poured out upon Jesus. We can glimpse this in verses such as Romans 5:9, "Much more then, having now been justified by His blood, we shall be saved from the wrath *of God* through Him," and Isaiah 53:10, which reads, "Yet it was the will of the LORD to crush Him; he has put Him to grief; when His <u>soul</u> makes an offering for guilt."

After His physical death, Jesus descended to Hell. Some find this offensive because Jesus was sinless and could never go to hell because He is God. They are, however, missing a few principles. The most obvious us that He was not paying for his sin but for ours. Also, for example, David penned in Psalm 139:8, "If I ascend to heaven, You are there; If I make my bed in Sheol, behold, You are there." Once again, He was making atonement for us by paying the fullness of the consequence we owed for sin. Yet, because Jesus was sinless, hell had no power to hold Him.

A Perspective on Paradise

There are a few verses I want us to look at to understand better what was going on. One is Luke 23:43, where Jesus spoke to the thief on the cross, stating, "Truly I say to you, today you will be with Me in Paradise."

There are only three times the word paradise is used in scripture. In Luke 23:43, 2 Corinthians 12:4, and Revelation 2:7. Theologians range in their understanding of how to interpret the word paradise. Some refer to the understanding of the Garden of Eden as the Garden of God, as paradise. The word has a Persian origin, "pairidoza" which means "a walled garden." Therefore, it is often assumed that the word paradise refers to a garden. The Septuagint, which is the Greek translation of the Old Testament, uses "paradiesos" in Genesis 2:8 to refer to the Garden of Eden. Seems to find agreement in our Revelation 2:7 passage which reads, "To him who overcomes, I will grant to eat of the tree of life which is in the Paradise of God." The Tree of Life is already known to be in the Garden of Eden. Genesis 3:24 teaches us this truth, "So He drove the man out, and at the east of the garden of Eden He stationed the cherubim and the flaming sword which turned every direction to guard the way to the tree of life." This correlation has a biblical root.

In the use of the word in 2 Corinthians 12:4, Paul describes being "caught up" to the third heaven. The verse provides a possible location for paradise, or at least what Paul described as paradise. If the Paradise referred to in Genesis and Revelation is earth-bound and the paradise Paul refers to is in the third heaven, then maybe different locations are referred to as paradise. Possibly the physical location of Paradise, the Garden, has changed. You will see why I mention this change of location in a moment.

In Luke, 16:19 we begin the account of Abraham's bosom. Whether it is a parable or a true account, we do not know for sure yet another issue that is debated as we all seek to understand more. There are theologians who would say that Abraham's Bosom is referring to heaven. They derive this from one of the statements used of the rich man where we read in Luke 16:22-23, "And the rich man also died and was buried. In Hades, where he was in torment, he looked up and saw Abraham from afar, with Lazarus by his side." Because of the statement, "he looked up" or "he raised his eyes," it is assumed that he was looking heavenward. I see the discomfort and hopelessness of the man causing him turmoil, and his eyes were downcast, looking toward his feet. To look up could just as easily indicate to raise his eyes from the ground. So, he looked up and saw across this chasm Abraham comforting Lazarus.

I want to state again that we do not have enough information written about this to know if it is a true account or whether it is simply a story. My explanation is based on what I put together from what we do know.

We do know that the only "payment" for sin is Jesus. His death was required for those who came after and those who came before. Jesus said in John 14:6, ""I am the way and the truth and the life. No one comes to the Father except through Me." Therefore, those who died prior to the payment of Jesus could not have gone to heaven. Paradise could not be in heaven or there would have existed another way to arrive in heaven other than through Jesus. If there was any other way, His sacrifice would have been for nothing. Prior to the death of Jesus, as the complete and satisfactory payment for sin, those who died in faith went to Abraham's Boson. They were those who died with faith in the promises of God and the coming Messiah. They lived by faith. Even though there had not yet been that propitiation, their faith had provided them a place of comfort while waiting for the Messiah.

Before Jesus died on the cross, hades was broken into two segments. One was a hell where torment existed for those who died without faith and waited for final judgment. After judgment, the eternal hell awaited, which would be much worse. Also, Abraham's Bosom is where those who died in faith found comfort while awaiting the sacrificial payment of the Messiah. I think it refers to the same place that we have seen, Abraham's bosom in Luke 16 above. For one, we know that Abraham's Bosom had a water source. Luke 16:24 reads, "Have mercy on me and send Lazarus to dip the tip of his finger in water and cool my tongue. For I am in agony in this fire." While any other source of comfort would be speculation, I assume the antithesis of his statement is that they were not in the fire, could comfort one another, and did not grow hungry. The assumption I would make from what we see written is that it was not a place of torment as it was across the chasm.

The place called Abrahams Bosom appears to have existed even prior to Abraham. It is taught in passages like Genesis 25:8 that when Abraham died, "He was gathered to his people." The implication is that he was gathered someplace. Even with the Prophet Samuel in 1 Samuel 28:14-15, Saul was surrounded by the Philistines, and Samuel was already dead. Saul was afraid and sought out a woman with a familiar spirit (demonic) from Endor to bring the spirit of Samuel back

KINGDOM AUTHORITY

to consult with Saul. We are told the spirit of Samuel came up out of the earth. The passage reads,

> "He said to her, "What is his form?" And she said, "An old man is coming up, and he is wrapped with a robe." And Saul knew that it was Samuel, and he bowed with his face to the ground and did homage. ¹⁵ Then Samuel said to Saul, "Why have you disturbed me by bringing me up?"

At that point in time, Samuel, a faithful prophet of God, "ascended up out of the earth" (1 Sam 28:13). Other words are used, such as "bring me up" and "cometh up." It would appear as if the place of comfort was a place from below. It was not as a garden on the earth or as a garden in heaven.

So, where do we find the correlation between the garden and Abraham's Bosom? Well, scripturally, it would only be the correlation made by Jesus to the thief on the cross from our Luke 23:43 passage, ""Truly I say to you, today you will be with Me in Paradise."

In the book of Ephesians 4:8-10, we read that Jesus descended into the lower parts of the earth. This statement agrees with great theologians like John McArthur that before his resurrection, Jesus descended into the lower parts and made a proclamation to the spirits now in prison. He writes," The demons may have been celebrating their seeming victory in the wake of Christ's death and burial—but only to soon be profoundly and permanently disappointed when the living Christ Himself arrived. The angelic spirits Christ was to address were now in prison." And "It was not to such unbound spirits, but to the bound demons that Christ went to announce His triumph." While his statements agree with the proclamation to the evil spirits in captivity, he does not appear to affirm the captive faithful.

Our Ephesians 4:8-10 passage reads, "*When he ascended on high, he led captivity captive, and gave gifts to people.*" Now this expression,

"He ascended," what does it mean except that He also had descended into the lower parts of the earth? He who descended is Himself also He who ascended far above all the heavens so that He might fill all things." Some would take the term "Lower parts of the earth to refer to the earth itself, but this is not a reference to the earth, it is a reference to the lower parts of the earth. The Hebrew word Sheol refers to a ravine or even a chasm, but it can also refer to the underworld or the place of the dead. We are told in Psalm 139:8, "If I ascend to heaven, You are there; If I make my bed in Sheol, behold, You are there." Therefore, we should not be surprised that Jesus could descend to even the earth's lowest parts. Shoel translates in Greek into Hades. In the book of 1 Peter we are told,

> "For Christ also died for sins once for all, the just for the unjust, so that He might bring us to God, having been put to death in the flesh, but made alive in the spirit; in which also **He went and made proclamation to the spirits now in prison**, who once were disobedient, when the patience of God kept waiting in the days of Noah, during the construction of the ark, in which a few, that is, eight persons, were brought safely through the water."

We had already addressed those disobedient spirits when we discussed Noah's days. The passage seems to confirm that Jesus descended and made a proclamation of victory. If these treacherous demons had sought to corrupt the genetic line of man so that the Seed of the Woman, the Messiah, could not save humanity, then I could understand the great relevance of this announcement. Jesus is saying, all of your plans, all of your scheming, have come to nothing.

We are also told in Ephesians 4:10 that "He led captivity captive." This is the part some theologians seem to forget. I believe He made a proclamation and then emptied Abraham's Bosom. Everyone who had died in faith now had the payment in full applied to their account. The penalty for their sin was paid. This entirety of the host of the faithful ascended to heaven at that time. Abraham's Bosom, or paradise, as a place, may have been relocated at that time. This could account for the later passages referring to Paradise in a heavenly direction.

Spiritual Gifts

We are also told that Jesus gave gifts to men when He ascended. Let's focus for a moment on the aspect of "giving gifts to people." We have looked at Ephesians 4:8-10. In the next two verses 11-12, we read, "And He gave some, apostles; and some, prophets; and some, evangelists; and some, pastors and teachers; For the perfecting of the saints, for the work of the ministry, for the edifying of the body of Christ."

The gifts that are poured out on the church are administered by the Holy Spirit, who was given later, on the day of Pentecost. This was essentially the birth of the church. Another area referring to spiritual gifts is found in 1 Corinthians 12:1-11.

> "Now concerning spiritual *gifts*, brethren, I do not want you to be unaware. ² You know that when you were pagans, *you were* led astray to the mute idols, however you were led. ³ Therefore I make known to you that no one speaking by the Spirit of God says, "Jesus is accursed"; and no one can say, "Jesus is Lord," except by the Holy Spirit. ⁴ Now there are varieties of gifts, but the same Spirit. ⁵ And there are varieties of ministries, and the same Lord. ⁶ There are varieties of effects, but the same God who works all things in all *persons*. ⁷ But to each one is given the manifestation of the Spirit for the common good. ⁸ For to one is given the word of wisdom through the Spirit, and to another the word of

> knowledge according to the same Spirit; [9] to another faith by the same Spirit, and to another gifts of healing by the one Spirit, [10] and to another the effecting of miracles, and to another prophecy, and to another the distinguishing of spirits, to another *various* kinds of tongues, and to another the interpretation of tongues. [11] But one and the same Spirit works all these things, distributing to each one individually just as He wills."

The second mentor the Lord brought into my life was the pastor at a church the Lord led me to attend in Puyallup, Washington. His name is Jay Chambers. I want to share with you how the Lord led me to the church because it encompasses many aspects, we have talked about in this book so far.

I had been a Christian for about four years, and while I tried several churches, I had not landed in what I would call a church home. I drove past this church in Puyallup almost every day. I was a smoker, and kitty-corner from the church was a small store. I would drive my motorcycle to the store to buy cigarettes. Every time I drove past this church, I felt like the Lord was speaking to my heart, telling me to go there. Sunday would come, and I would wake up and hear the Lord speak to my heart, saying, "Get up and go." Week after week, I would say, "I will go next week." This happened for about a month, and Sunday rolled around again. I woke up and could hear the Lord tell me to go. I gave my usual response of saying, next Sunday, and it was like the Lord's spirit said, "NO, NOW!" I did not expect that, and I got up and got ready and went. I had no idea what time the service started, but I went. I got there early for service and met a few people who invited me to help fold bulletins for the coming service. I have to tell you, from the moment I walked into that church. I felt like I was home. I had never felt that before.

Whereas through Roger Donald, the Lord worked on my obedience through my submission to the authority of the Bible, God used

Jay for a different purpose. It was through Jay that the Lord taught me to pray and worship. Jay became my prayer partner, and we would meet in the morning at the church to pray together. While I felt I had a good relationship with the Lord, it was through this time my relationship with God started to deepen even more, and I began to understand surrender in a new way, and through surrender, to understand what it actually meant to worship. It was at this church I felt my call to the ministry. This, of course, brings us back to gifts.

One of the things that Jay taught me I want to share with you. Spiritual gifts fall into essentially three categories: Managerial, Ministerial, and Manifestation. Regardless of where you stand on the use or existence of manifestational gifts today, these categories made sense to me then and still do today.

We are told in John 14:26, "But the Comforter, which is the Holy Ghost, whom the Father will send in my name, He shall teach you all things, and bring all things to your remembrance, whatsoever I have said unto you. In John 16:7, we read, "Nevertheless, I tell you the truth; It is expedient for you that I go away: for if I go not away, the Comforter will not come unto you; but if I depart, I will send Him unto you."

It is worthy to note that in the Ephesians 4:11-12 passage, Jesus is the one who gives the gifts. In Corinthians 12:11, we are told the Spirit gives spiritual gifts. But the fullness is earlier in Corinthians 12:4-6, "⁴ There are different kinds of gifts, but the same **Spirit** distributes them. ⁵ There are different kinds of service, but the same **Lord**. ⁶ There are different kinds of working, but in all of them and in everyone, it is the same **God** at work." We can see that the trinity's fullness is involved in working out of our spiritual gifts.

After Jesus' bodily resurrection, we know that He told Mary that He had not yet ascended. The group that believed Jesus simply went to heaven when He died might state that Jesus came back down into his resurrected body and had not yet ascended again to the Father at the time He met with Mary. Read what Mary experienced in John 20:1-17

"Now on the first day of the week Mary Magdalene came early to the tomb, while it was still dark, and saw the stone already taken away from the tomb. So she ran and came to Simon Peter and to the other disciple whom Jesus loved, and said to them, "They have taken away the Lord out of the tomb, and we do not know where they have laid Him." So Peter and the other disciple went forth, and they were going to the tomb. The two were running together, and the other disciple ran ahead faster than Peter and came to the tomb first; and stooping and looking in, he saw the linen wrappings lying there; but he did not go in. And so Simon Peter also came, following him, and entered the tomb; and he saw the linen wrappings lying there, and the face-cloth which had been on His head, not lying with the linen wrappings, but rolled up in a place by itself. So the other disciple who had first come to the tomb then also entered, and he saw and believed. For as yet they did not understand the Scripture, that He must rise again from the dead. So the disciples went away again to their own homes."

But Mary was standing outside the tomb weeping; and so, as she wept, she stooped and looked into the tomb; and she saw two angels in white sitting, one at the head and one at the feet, where the body of Jesus had been lying. And they said to her, "Woman, why are you weeping?" She said to them, "Because they have taken away my Lord, and I do not know where they have laid Him." When she had said this, she turned around and saw Jesus standing there, and did not know that it was Jesus. Jesus said to her, "Woman, why are you weeping? Whom are you seeking?" Supposing Him

> *to be the gardener, she said to Him, "Sir, if you have carried Him away, tell me where you have laid Him, and I will take Him away." Jesus said to her, "Mary!" She turned and said to Him in Hebrew, "Rabboni!" (which means, Teacher). Jesus said to her, "Stop clinging to Me, for I have not yet ascended to the Father; but go to My brethren and say to them,*

I believe that Jesus was speaking clearly and that He had not yet ascended to the Father. The main thing I want you to consider here is, does it matter? Ultimately, no. It does not. What matters is that we try and use scripture to interpret scripture. Sometimes that takes a bit of work. There is something we call a hermeneutical spiral. The hermeneutical spiral simply means that every time we come into a passage of scripture, we go into it with more than before. To reuse the puzzle example, the second time I build a puzzle, the easier it is to build because I understand it.

The big idea conveyed is that when Jesus died on the cross, He descended into Abrahams's bosom, Paradise, and made a proclamation of his victory, and led free those who were held captive. He was resurrected into a physical body and ascended into heaven. The Holy Spirit was given to the church as a seal of our promised inheritance, and spiritual gifts were poured out upon its members.

The last thing I want to say here is that spiritual gifts for the building up of the body of Christ, which is the church. Hopefully, this brings about the awareness that the church is something we should be taking part in. The church is a place that can help us to learn so that we can identify our spiritual gifts and begin serving in the church. The church is not a place to go and get your needs met. It is a place where you go to meet the needs of others. In doing this, we will find our needs met.

Triune nature of prayer

One of the most remarkable aspects of prayer, like spiritual gifts, is that the fullness of the Trinity is involved in our prayer life. In Matthew 6:9, we are directed to pray to the Father, "Pray, then, in this way: 'Our Father, who is in heaven, Hallowed be Your name." Jesus also tells us in John 14:13 to ask in his name. "And whatever you ask in My name, this I will do, so that the Father may be glorified in the Son." We find in Ephesians 6:18 this instruction, "pray at all times in the Spirit." Or in Jude 1:20, "But you, beloved, building yourselves up on your most holy faith, praying in the Holy Spirit," So, we pray to the Father in the Son's name, and we pray in the Spirit.

Prayer is incredibly powerful. When speaking of prayer here, I am referring to the prayers of a Christian to our loving God. More important than prayer is to whom you pray. As stated above, the whole of the Trinity is involved in our prayer life but let's go deeper.

While God is in ultimate authority over everything, this world is under the authority of the enemy of God. It has been cast into spiritual darkness. The most important way for God to accomplish His will in this kingdom of darkness is for those who dwell here to accomplish it. God works through the lives of His people to accomplish his will. That is why we are ambassadors for Christ as we are told in 2 Corinthians 5:20, "We are therefore Christ's ambassadors, as though God were making his appeal through us. We implore you on Christ's behalf: Be reconciled to God." That is why He sends us forth. We are to carry on the mission that Jesus started. Matthew 28:18-20, *"Therefore go and make disciples of all nations, baptizing them in the name of the Father and of the Son and of the Holy Spirit, [20] and teaching them to obey everything I have commanded you. And surely I am with you always, to the very end of the age."* That is the way the kingdom of light operates in the kingdom of darkness. When we pray, we are inviting the will of God to operate on earth as it is in heaven. Matthew 6:19, *"Your kingdom come. Your will be done, on earth as it is in heaven."*

We are in a unique position. We are inhabitants of both kingdoms. We were physically born and live in the kingdom of darkness, and yet, we are citizens of the kingdom of light. When we, as believers, pray, we are inviting God to work in this kingdom of darkness through us. Isn't this the very idea Jesus taught in the Lord's prayer, "Thy kingdom come, they will be done, on earth as it is in heaven."

However, we must remember that effective prayer cannot effectively be accomplished in the flesh. It will not produce anything of real value, especially if there is unconfessed sin in our lives. We must pray at all times in the spirit.

One of the most incredible aspects of the Christian life is that we are not here to live in this world and to be distracted by it. We are here in this world for the purpose of reaching those still trapped in darkness with the message of salvation. Remember, if they die under the authority of the adversary, they will bear the consequence of their own sin and suffer an eternity with the adversary. They will take part in his judgment and his torment. This punishment was never for them. We are told it was for Satan and his angels (fallen), Matthew 25:41, "Then He will also say to those on His left, 'Depart from Me, you accursed people, into the eternal fire which has been prepared for the devil and his angels.'"

Through prayer, we who are citizens of light seek to maintain a right relationship with God. We are children of the kingdom of light, yet, as those living in the kingdom of darkness, it is somewhat impossible not to be infected by the sin it carries with it. God is aware of this and provides a way for us to be cleansed. If we do not, the darkness continues to drag us farther and farther away from God. Our hearts may become so seared by the callousness of sin that we turn our backs on the very faith by which we are saved.

We have looked Romans 6:12-14 reads,

> "Therefore do not let sin reign in your mortal body so that you obey its lusts, [13] and do not go on presenting the members of your body to sin *as* instruments of unrighteousness; but present yourselves to God as those alive from the dead, and your members *as* instruments of righteousness to God. [14] For sin shall not be master over you, for you are not under law but under grace."

We have to walk in our Christian life with a measure of discernment over our choices. Romans 12:1-2 tells us,

> "Therefore I urge you, brethren, by the mercies of God, to present your bodies a living and holy sacrifice, acceptable to God, *which is* your spiritual service of worship. [2] And do not be conformed to this world, but be transformed by the renewing of your mind, so that you may prove what the will of God is, that which is good and acceptable and perfect."

Now one of the most remarkable truths about prayer is that it can have a real impact as we invite God to work out his plan in the world around us and through us. I remember standing in the doorway of a hospital room talking with a doctor. The unconscious woman in the room was the mother of one of my congregation members. The doctor told me she would not make it through the day and probably not more than a few more hours. Even though she was unconscious, I went in and held her hand. I felt the Lord asking me to pray for her. So, holding her right hand with my right hand, I placed my left hand on her forehead, and I prayed that God would heal her according to his will. It was one of the moments where you know your prayer was effective and

God heard your prayer, some of you know what I mean. This woman was in church the following Sunday. I did not tell many about what I had done praying for her because it was not about me, and I certainly did not heal her. This was a God thing. God healed her to accomplish whatever purpose He had in mind. Certainly, I have prayed for more people to be healed than I have seen healed, but prayer invites God to work in this kingdom of darkness. So, the question is, how do we have a powerful prayer life?

Here is your answer. Scripture teaches us that the prayers of a righteous man (person) accomplish much, as we read in James 5:16. "The effective prayer of a righteous man can accomplish much." Unfortunately, we are also told Romans 3:10, "There is none righteous, no, not one." It seems almost funny. Wait, the only way to have effective prayer is to be righteous, but no one is righteous! The answer is found in 1 John 1:7-10, " But if we walk in the light, as He is in the light, we have fellowship one with another, and the blood of Jesus Christ His Son cleanseth us from all sin. If we say that we have no sin, we deceive ourselves, and the truth is not in us. If we confess our sins, He is faithful and just to forgive our sins and cleanse us from all unrighteousness. If we say that we have not sinned, we make Him a liar, and his word is not in us."

We can see that the passages teach us that we can be cleansed from all unrighteousness. If we are cleansed from all unrighteousness, how much unrighteousness remains? If you answered none, then you are correct! When I pray, I come humbly and honestly before the Lord, and I ask Him to forgive me for those sins that I know I have committed. I also ask Him to forgive me where I may have sinned that I may not be aware. I want to be right before God. If sin destroyed my relationship with the Lord in the first place, the last thing I want to do is to fall back into sin. I do not want to hinder my relationship with my Lord. Likewise, I want my prayers to produce results.

More can be said about prayer. Many books have been written on the subject. I wanted to hit a few important truths in regard to prayer to move us in the right direction to experience a powerful prayer life. I would encourage further study because there is much more in the Bible about prayer. The main takeaway now is that **the prayers of the righteous have real results**, we are unrighteous people. Our first step is to prayer that God will forgive us for our sins and cleanse us from all of our unrighteousness, then as one righteous, we make our requests known. Again, much more can be said but what I stated here is powerful and effective.

Study of the Word of God -The Path

For the Christian to experience victory as a Child of the Kingdom of Light while living in the Kingdom of Darkness, the most important truth is understanding that we must stay in the Word of God. Scripture tells us in Psalm 119:105, "Thy Word is a lamp unto my feet and a light unto my path." Picture the idea of walking along a path. While you are on it, you can see the path. The light reveals it to you, and you can stay on the path a few steps at a time because the light illuminates only so far ahead.

When I was growing up, bouncing between parents, I lived for a time during my High School years up in White Pass, Washington. My mother and stepfather owned a little grocery store and gas station up in the mountains. Nearby there was a ranger station camp with cabins. Over the summer, they would have work crews coming in, and the crews would live in these cabins. They would spend the summer doing stuff like trail maintenance. We would always get to know the crews because they would shop at our store. My stepbrother and I would hang out and spend time over at the cabins. If I stayed over visiting too late, I would walk back to our house on the trail, through the woods, in the dark. Luckily, I had a flashlight because the path was dark and impossible to see in the trees. Many times, even with the flashlight, I would find myself veering to the left or right. In the same way, the flashlight helped me to stay on the trail; the word of God helps us navigate this kingdom of darkness.

We have to remember there is nothing profitable out there in the darkness. There is nothing that is profitable to the child of light, and if you veer far enough off the path, it can be hard to find your way back. The child of light must understand there is only one way to navigate our way through the darkness, and that is with the light of the Word of God illuminating our path before us. If we go to the left or to the right, we have been tempted to ignore the counsel of scripture in the same way that Adam and Eve did in the beginning. But if we study the Word and hide it in our hearts, we will know how to respond to the temptations the darkness presents. David teaches us from Psalm 119:11, "Your Word have I hidden in my heart that I might not sin against you."

This is where sin comes into play. Sin is veering to the left or right of the path. It moves us into the darkness. Even a lie in the life of a child of God moves us off the path into the darkness, and the farther we go, the harder it is to find our way back.

Sin always leads to darkness. It is deceptive and can seem to have value to us. Of course, it does. The one thing about temptation is that it is tempting. As with Adam and Eve, the enemy can make something evil appear to be for our good, and it can be difficult to see it for what it is. We might even try to convince ourselves that our choice is actually of the light. We must recognize that seeking to justify what the Word tells us is a sin should reveal that we are already off the path and walking into the darkness. Repentance brings us back to the path, and rebellion leads us farther into the darkness.

Now, in this conversation of authority, we have to understand that we experience victory as believers while we are walking on the path illuminated by the Word of God. In other words, we are walking under the authority of the Bible. Second, we must understand that when we veer off the path and step into the darkness, this sin allows the enemy of God legal authority to attack us. We become vulnerable. Legally vulnerable to his attacks.

The darkness and the things that lie within the darkness call out to us. They try to get us to walk off the path and step back into the darkness where we used to live. As I mentioned, the problem with temptation is that it is tempting. We have to remember what it was like when we lived there. In the midst of temptation, we may even begin to romanticize some of the sins that once infected us.

I remember how different I felt when I came to know Jesus as my Lord. I felt so different. But as time went on, I started to wonder if I really felt different. In talking with the Lord about this, He would give me what I call flashes of secularism. It only happened a few times, and it only would last a second, but it was an overwhelming feeling. It was the emptiness that I felt before I knew Jesus. It was such a painful emptiness I could not believe that this was normal for me prior to knowing Jesus. Not a part of me ever wants to feel that way again. The Lord made it evident that I was no longer of the world. I was now his child.

As believers, as children of light, sin can entangle us. The enemy can entangle our minds to such a degree that we are no longer seeking the path. This is especially confusing when we start listening to the voices of those walking near the edge of the path calling for us to join them. Some of which might also be the church. When we take our eyes off the path and begin looking into the darkness, we have made the first mistake. Scripture teaches us 2 Corinthians 6:14, "For what do righteousness and wickedness have in common? Or what fellowship can light have with darkness? In the same way, light seeks to dispel the darkness; darkness is always encroaching on the light. Anytime the light dims, the darkness expands its kingdom.

There is no doubt that walking as a child of the kingdom of light can be lonely as we traverse the kingdom of darkness. It is nothing like the loneliness I felt walking in the darkness with others, apart from Jesus. We must recognize that our eyes are on the wrong relationship when we are enticed by the darkness or enticed by those within the darkness. Hebrews 13:5 reads, "Let your conversation be without covetousness; and be content with such things as ye have: for He hath said, I will never leave thee, nor forsake thee." We must understand two truths: real fellowship comes as we stay on the path. Two, we can experience this real fellowship which is found in the cure for those times when we veer off the path. Once again, the cure is found in 1 John 1:6-10 reads,

> "[6] If we say that we have fellowship with Him and *yet* walk in the darkness, we lie and do not practice the truth; [7] but if we walk in the Light as He Himself is in the Light, we have fellowship with one another, and the blood of Jesus His Son cleanses us from all sin. [8] If we say that we have no sin, we are deceiving ourselves and the truth is not in us. [9] If we confess our sins, He is faithful and righteous to forgive us our sins and to cleanse us from all unrighteousness. [10] If we say that we have not sinned, we make Him a liar, and His word is not in us."

We experience real fellowship with God and even other believers when we are walking the path. We must allow the Word of God to illuminate the path we are on and teach us to practice discernment to help us know when we are off the path. We must see it for what it is and acknowledge the truth by confessing the darkness for what it really is and returning to the path.

The worst part about compromising and walking into the darkness by veering to the side of the path is that it confuses those seeking the real path. To be clear here, it is confusing to those seeking Jesus. Those still in the darkness draw close to us, seeking a way out of the darkness, and we become obstacles for them. They cannot see the beauty of the path because the children of light, are found walking in darkness. We will never experience victory in this way and the potentially worse result is that we may hinder others from being set free from the darkness. We must return to the path. It is only on the path we find fellowship with one another and real fellowship with God. Matthew 7:14 reads, "For the gate is small, and the way is narrow that leads to life."

I have met so many believers that tell me they once felt so close in their relationship with God, and now they feel so far away from Him. I get it. I have gone through periods in my life feeling the same way. Once I felt I was able to speak to God and hear Him speak to me. At other times I realized that I could not hear Him speak. I even started to wonder if I had really felt that close to God or if it was in my imagination. But please hear this. You did not imagine it. The intimacy that you once felt with God is real, and you can experience this relationship again. To do so, you must return to the path. You may have heard this before, "God is never the one who walks away."

Learning to listen

You have heard me speak about hearing the Lord. There are two ways we can hear the voice of the Lord. One and the most common is internal, and the second is external. Again, externally is one area that many will tell you does not happen, but they are wrong. Because they have not had the experience does not mean it does not occur.

I was going through a tough time in my early Christian walk with the Lord. I will share with you some of what I was going through. I want to preempt this by telling you that this was one of the situations my first mentor Roger Donald, told me I should not be in. I did not listen, and the results were horrible. The following was the result.

I made a lot of mistakes as a young, un-discipled, and undisciplined believer, but God was growing me. I was in a relationship I should not have been in, living with my girlfriend. She broke up with me, and since she was pregnant, I let her have our apartment, and I moved out. Finding myself homeless, I lived in my car. During this time, I ended up having a tooth pulled, and the dentist broke into my sinus cavity, which resulted in surgery. I ended up with twenty-two stitches on the roof of my mouth, and I was unable to eat for two weeks. I had my belongings in the car with me, so with little room, the only way I could sleep was to lean the driver's seat back as far as it would go and try to get some sleep. Every night I would wake up to the police knocking on my window and asking why I was sleeping in my car. They would tell me I was not allowed to sleep in the parking lot I was parked in, and I would have to move along. There were times they would have compassion; they would let me finish the night where I was but tell me to find somewhere else the next night.

I had friends who would tell me that they could not believe how well I was doing, considering everything I was going through. My friends did not see me when I was alone at night in my car. One night I was crying out to the Lord. I said that I felt like every time I started getting back on my feet, it was like someone would pull the rug out from under me, and I would fall. Then as if sitting next to me in the passenger seat, I heard this voice say, "I will not let you fall." You might think I would have been in shock, I was not, I felt at peace. I fell asleep feeling at peace. Three days later, I was again crying out to the Lord, saying," Okay, you're not letting me fall. How far will you let me fall before you catch me!" This was the only time I have heard the voice of the Lord audibly. As we walk with the Lord, I want us to understand that we are not alone. We are filled with His spirit, and we have a personal connection. The Lord knows what we are going through, and he will meet us where we are. He will never leave us nor forsake us!

Why did God choose to speak to me then at that moment? I do not know for sure. I do know I had already picked a date to leave the world. Hearing the Lord speak to me did not just bring me comfort. It changed my whole direction. I want you to know something very real for me during that time. Even though I was making terrible choices, I was seeking the Lord. I was insincere in prayer and study of his word on a daily basis for no other reason than to know Him better. I honestly wanted to know God more personally.

I recently met with one of my mentors, and he told me that he always remembered how I refer to God as "Father," not "our Father." That was something I never noticed or thought about. I have always sought God as my Father. I believe we all have this relationship with Him whereby we can call out "Abba Father" which means daddy father. Jesus used this term in Mark 14:36 when He said, "And He was saying, "Abba! Father! All things are possible for You; remove this cup from Me; yet not what I will, but what You *will*." Paul imparted this idea to believers in Romans 8:15, "For you have not received a spirit of slavery leading to fear again, but you have received a spirit of adoption as sons *and daughters* by which we cry out, "Abba! Father!" Then in Galatians 4:6, "Because you are sons, God has sent the Spirit of His Son into our hearts, crying out, "Abba! Father!" I believe the Lord loves us so much that we come to Him, and He will embrace us as would a loving father. I have always believed this.

We know that scripture supports the Lord talking to us. Maybe He has spoken to you too. Praise God. We know He spoke to Samuel in 1 Samuel 3:1-14,

> *"Samuel served the LORD by helping Eli the priest, who was by that time almost blind. In those days, the LORD hardly ever spoke directly to people, and he did not appear to them in dreams very often. But one night, Eli was asleep in his room, ³ and Samuel was sleeping on a mat near the sacred chest in the LORD's house. They had not been asleep very long ⁴ when the LORD called out Samuel's name. "Here I am!" Samuel answered. ⁵ Then he ran to Eli and said, "Here I am. What do you want?" "I didn't call you," Eli answered. "Go back to bed." Samuel went back. ⁶ Again the LORD called out Samuel's name. Samuel got up and went to Eli. "Here I am," he said. "What do you want?" Eli told him, "Son, I didn't call you. Go back to sleep." ⁷ The LORD had not*

spoken to Samuel before, and Samuel did not recognize the voice. [8] When the LORD called out his name for the third time, Samuel went to Eli again and said, "Here I am. What do you want?" Eli finally realized that it was the LORD who was speaking to Samuel. [9] So he said, "Go back and lie down! If someone speaks to you again, answer, 'I'm listening, LORD. What do you want me to do?'" Once again Samuel went back and lay down. [10] The LORD then stood beside Samuel and called out as he had done before, "Samuel! Samuel!" "I'm listening," Samuel answered. "What do you want me to do?" [11] The LORD said: Samuel, I am going to do something in Israel that will shock everyone who hears about it! [12] I will punish Eli and his family, just as I promised. [13] He knew that his sons refused to respect me, and he let them get away with it, even though I said I would punish his family forever. [14] I warned Eli that sacrifices or offerings could never make things right! His family has done too many disgusting things."

Of course, God not only spoke to Moses but showed up in a burning bush. With Abraham, He not only spoke but walked with Him and ate with Him. Believe me when I tell you I am not comparing myself to the mighty servants of God from the Bible. I am a sinner saved by God's grace, and the only thing I seem to succeed at is failing God. I wish I could have a conversation with the Lord. An audible back and forth conversation. My comfort is in knowing one hundred percent that God loves us and walks with us. He will never leave us nor forsake us. Even when we are making horrible choices and suffering the consequence of those choices as I was at the time.

One caution I would make in this area is to practice discernment. The Lord is never going to call us to do something contrary to scripture.

Meditating on the Word

Listening for the voice of the Lord comes from more than just reading the Bible and praying. It certainly encompasses those too. We definitely, need to "study to show ourselves approved before God workman, not needing to be ashamed but rightly dividing the Word of truth." (2 Tim2:15). We also need to be praying without ceasing. (1 Thes 5:17). The main two things I have discovered that go along with prayer and study are meditating on the Word of the Lord and [key point] seeking to maintain a heart that genuinely desires to be obedient to the leading and guiding of the Lord. The more I am in communion with the Lord throughout my day, the more I learn to discern his voice through all of the noise of this world. We learn to listen for that still, quiet voice that can speak so loudly from within us through these practices.

How can God speak to us? He does this through the spirit of man. Remembering we are body, soul, and spirit, God can connect with individuals to accomplish his purpose in this world of darkness. As I mentioned before, mankind is unique in this way. We connect with this world through the flesh and the spiritual realm through the spirit. Some being wired closer to the veil and can discern the spiritual realm differently. There is also the truth that God sends his spirit into the world to convict a man of sin, righteousness, and the coming judgment. (John 16:7-8). His living spirit will speak to the spirit of humans. It is for us to respond. Think of it like God is making a phone call. Will you answer the phone?

There are also those who seek after the true and living God. God is able to speak to their spirit and guide them. We see God reaching down and speaking to these people throughout the scriptures. Noah, Abraham, Moses, and the list goes on. God works through these people to accomplish his will. This may have something to do with the genetics we spoke of before, or it may simply be a spiritual issue because it is the spirit that closely connects us with God as it is the flesh that closely connects us to the world. If some are predisposed to the spirit, it may be easier to hear the Lord, as I have mentioned previously. It might be because they had humble and contrite hearts truly seeking God.

I want us to see and understand, and I want to be clear on this. God is able to work in this kingdom of darkness through those people who are faithful to His calling and obedient to what He asks them to do. It is by faith that they walked with God, and that same faith by which we walk with God now. In the Old Testament, the Spirit of God would rest on a person. Today every true believer is alive in the spirit and has the unique ability to connect with God in this living Spirit. The Holy Spirit of God makes the believer in the Lord Jesus alive in the spirit. It is like having a "ten G" cell phone on you at all times, not with God on speed dial, but with the line already open.

Once again, we have to understand that sin is the only barrier between man and God. Once the issue of sin has been dealt with through the payment of Jesus and applied to our sin debt, we are free from entanglement to any sins previously committed. We have a free, unfettered relationship with the creator, God.

I stated this in the above way for a reason. A believer can become entangled in sin again. Sin will affect their relationship with God. Sin can entangle the believer to the point that it can seem as if they are no longer saved. The good news is that God knew in advance that we would struggle with entanglement in the world. After all, we live our lives in this corrupted world and in a body of flesh that is still enticed by the sin in the world. Our flesh is still corrupted, so this entanglement is to be expected. But we also need to understand that this is no excuse to remain in sin.

It is here I want to talk about victory over this entanglement. We already have victory over sin. That was found in the Lord, who is Jesus, the Christ. What we are talking about now comes into the realm of being a disciple of Jesus. This is where the work comes in. Being a believer in Jesus is not simply about saying a prayer and getting on with your life. It is found in understanding the great consequence of sin. And recognizing the extent to which God was willing to go so that we might be saved, rescued from sin. It is learning to take away the priority that sin once held in our lives. Sin held us in bondage to Satan and the death we owed for sin. We do not have to walk in the way of this world any longer. We have been set free. Now we can learn to walk in the freedom that we have. We can walk in the freedom of life in the Spirit. Walking in this way is both incredible and exciting. Even though we physically still live in the same kingdom of darkness, trapped in a body prone to sin, we are no longer citizens of that kingdom. We have been taken out from under Satan's authority; We now have the freedom to live as citizens of a different kingdom, the kingdom of light. We live under the authority of Jesus, our Christ.

Life is literally different now that Jesus has come. We are taught that Jesus came into this world of darkness as Light. We are taught this in scripture. John 1:4-5, "⁴In Him was life, and the life was the Light of men. ⁵The Light shines in the darkness, and the darkness did not comprehend it." In the same way that sin brought in death, the kingdom of darkness is built on this death, that eternal separation from God. Jesus brought in life which is itself the light of men. It is the light of a new life in the spirit. We who have been made alive again in Christ have something new and distinct.

As a believer, we have the reunited relationship with God that Adam and Eve lost in the beginning. It is a restored imperfect relationship. It is imperfect because we still experience the world around us through our flesh. Yet, we are still alive in Christ. Colossians 1:27-29 reads,

> "To whom God willed to make known what is the riches of the glory of this mystery among the Gentiles, which is Christ in you, the hope of glory. We proclaim Him, admonishing every man and teaching every man with all wisdom, so that we may present every

man complete in Christ. For this purpose also I labor, striving according to His power, which mightily works within me."

We have the indwelling of the Spirit within us. It sets us apart from the rest of the world as those who are alive in Christ." Tie this in with 1 Peter 2:9, in which we are told, "that ye should show forth the praises of Him who hath called you out of darkness into His marvelous light."

Now maybe you can get a glimpse into the change that has taken place in the life of a believer in the Lord Jesus Christ. We are no longer dead in the spirit but alive. We need to walk in this new life in the Spirit. The relationship we have been created to have with God exists. The difficulty we have is putting aside the things of the flesh to experience life in the spirit. I have so often told my congregations that we would never sin if we were able to walk by the spirit one hundred percent of the time. The problem is that we lived according to the flesh, apart from the spirit, for a duration of time prior to knowing Jesus. The world itself is contrary to the things of the spirit, and we are in a spiritual war that we continue to fight. So now it is an ongoing battle that is overcome through continuous study of scripture, prayer, meditating on scriptures, and walking in submission to the authority of the Lord, as we learn to distinguish the sound of the spirit of God speaking to our spirit. If we can learn to hear God speak to our spirit, then chances are we are walking in the spirit.

THE MOST IMPORTANT KEY TO WALKING IN THE SPIRIT IS TO REALIZE WE ARE UNDER THE AUTHORITY OF CHRIST. The enemy no longer has authority over us. We have to walk in our freedom. Many Christians live their lives with Stockholm Syndrome. They still walk in the same bondage they were in prior to Jesus. This is where discipleship comes in. We are to make disciples, not converts.

Listen to this passage in Romans 8:6-8, "For the mind set on the flesh is death, but the mind set on the Spirit is life and peace, because the mind set on the flesh is hostile toward God; for it does not subject itself to the law of God, for it is not even able to do so, and those who are in the flesh cannot please God."

So how do we overcome this body of flesh that is prone to sin? Galatians 5:16-17 provides an answer,

> *"So I say, walk by the Spirit, and you will not gratify the desires of the flesh. For the flesh craves what is contrary to the Spirit, and the Spirit what is contrary to the flesh. They are opposed to each other, so that you do not do what you want."*

Remember what we are told in Romans 8:3, "For what the Law could not do, weak as it was through the flesh, God did: sending His own Son in the likeness of sinful flesh and as an offering for sin, He **condemned sin in the flesh**." Galatians 5:24 reads, "Now those who belong to Christ Jesus have crucified the flesh with its passions and desires. In reality, sin is trapped in our flesh. Our flesh relates to the world, and it is has been corrupted by sin. There is no hope for our bodies marred by sin. This is why we are going to get a new body, a resurrected body. Read 1 Corinthians 15:50-58,

> *"Now I declare to you, brothers, that flesh and blood cannot inherit the kingdom of God, nor does the perishable inherit the imperishable. Listen, I tell you a mystery: We will not all sleep, but we will all be changed— in an instant, in the twinkling of an eye, at the last trumpet. For the trumpet will sound, the dead will be raised imperishable, and we will be changed. For the perishable must be clothed with the imperishable, and the mortal with immortality. When the perishable has been clothed with the imperishable and the mortal with immortality, then the saying that is written will come to pass: "Death has been swallowed up in victory.*

> "Where, O Death, is your victory? Where, O Death, is your sting? The sting of death is sin, and the power of sin is the law. But thanks be to God, who gives us the victory through our Lord Jesus Christ! Therefore, my beloved brothers, be steadfast and immovable. Always excel in the work of the Lord, because you know that your labor in the Lord is not in vain."

One of the most amazing truths about the authority of God is that God is able to work out his plan in spite of the wicked plans of the enemy. Satan has not laid one plan that has found God unaware. His plans will avail nothing. To be clear, God is ultimately sovereign, and He has all power and all authority, but he will not circumvent the laws he has created. Satan has authority over this world. God has worked within the laws He has created and has brought about our salvation regardless of the devil's wicked schemes.

The believer in the Lord Jesus has a part to play in the plan of God. We must realize this to fulfill our purpose. We need to understand this to fulfill the mission that God has called us to be a part of. There are people still trapped in the darkness who need to come to understand who Jesus is.

The Question, the Believer, and the Church

When we are speaking of the church, we begin in Matthew 16:13-19, where Jesus asks a question of his disciples,

> "Who do people say that the Son of Man is?" And they said, "Some say John the Baptist; and others, Elijah; but still others, Jeremiah, or one of the prophets." He said to them, "But who do you say that I am?" Simon Peter answered, "You are the Christ, the Son of the living God." And Jesus said to him, "Blessed are you, Simon

AUTHORITY OF FOLLOWERS OF JESUS

> *Barjona, because flesh and blood did not reveal this to you, but My Father who is in heaven. "I also say to you that you are Peter, and upon this Rock I will build My Church; and the gates of Hades will not overpower it. "I will give you the keys of the kingdom of heaven; and whatever you bind on earth shall have been bound in heaven, and whatever you loose on earth ²shall have been loosed in heaven."⁵*

We need to understand several foundational truths from this passage about the church and what it means to build a church. The vital question we must all understand is, who is Jesus? So, if this is the preceding question, then we know that this is the foundation upon which everything else in the conversation is built. So, the church's foundation is not just Jesus, but it is who Jesus is.

There is some controversy about what the passage is saying. Is it teaching that Peter is the foundation of the church? The answer is no. The church is built upon the confession of Peter when he answers, "You are the Christ, the son of the living God." This distinction is seen when we understand the original Greek for Petros (Πέτρος) and petra (πέτρα). In Greek, Petros is a small stone or a type of small Rock that can be thrown. It does not have any stability, but petra, is a mountain, sometimes translated as a mountain range. It is a big rock, a firm foundation. It is upon the strong foundation that the church is built. Listen to these words again; after Peter Says Jesus is the Christ the Son of the Living God, Jesus says, *"Blessed are you, Simon Barjona, because flesh and blood did not reveal this to you, but My Father who is in heaven." "You are Peter (Petros, the small stone). It is upon this Rock (Petra, firm foundation) that confession you just made of Jesus, I will build my church."* So why do some find confusion and think Peter is the foundation of the church. They do not understand the distinction of these

---

⁵ New American Standard Bible: 1995 Update (La Habra, CA: The Lockman Foundation, 1995),Mk 16:13-19. All further references from the bible

words, and they are not considering the full context of the passage. They see that Peter is blessed, and they read that he is given the keys to the kingdom of heaven. Is Peter foundational to the church? Yes, but he is not the foundation of the church. In reality, the foundation of the church is not even the confession, but it is what the confession teaches, that Jesus is the Christ, the son of the living God. It is not even that Jesus is the foundation of the church. It is that Jesus is the Christ. Jesus is the Son of the Living God. Jesus is the savior, He is the Messiah. This is the foundation of the church. Ekklesia is the Greek word for the church. It means the called out ones. While it can refer to any group of called out citizens it is used in reference to the church. Remember we have been called out of the darkness and brought into his marvelous light.

I want to share a couple of other truths from this passage with us. We know what keys do. Keys open things. They provide access. Peter was the first one to receive the keys that provided access. Not at the point of confession, for Jesus says, "I <u>will</u> give you" speaking of a time in the future.

Peter would not be the only one. We have to ask why he will receive these keys. He received them because he recognized the truth of whom Jesus is and made a confession of this truth. If heaven for a time was shut up, and we could not access heaven due to our sin, this confession is the key to the kingdom of heaven.

Next, we need to understand the idea of authority. I want us to recognize the progression that we see here. Peter's confession is the key, and the key gains him legal access to the kingdom of heaven. The legal access to the kingdom through the confession imparts power. He has authority through the confession to enter heaven's kingdom and the power to operate as a representative of the kingdom of heaven here on earth. Peter did not steal the keys to the kingdom of heaven. We are told, "Whatever you bind on earth will be bound in heaven, and whatever you lose on earth will be loosed in heaven." We see the pouring out of authority and power. Because Peter was the first does not mean Peter was the only. 1 Corinthians 12:3 reads, "Therefore I make known to you that no one speaking by the Spirit of God says, "Jesus is accursed"; and no one can say, "Jesus is Lord," except by the Holy Spirit."

I would put before you that the confession that Jesus is the Lord is indeed the key to accessing heaven. Romans 10-9 reads, "if you confess with your mouth Jesus *as* Lord, and believe in your heart that God raised Him from the dead, you will be saved." Jesus Himself teaches us in John 14:6, "I am the way, and the truth, and the life; no one comes to the Father but through Me." Again, Jesus said in John10:7,

> *"So Jesus said to them again, "Truly, truly, I say to you, I am the door of the sheep. "All who came before Me are thieves and robbers, but the sheep did not hear them. "I am the door; if anyone enters through Me, he will be saved, and will go in and out and find pasture.*

By putting these truths together, we can understand that Jesus is the door or gate. The confession that Jesus is the Christ is the key. Jesus asks each of us that same question today. Whom do you say that I am? We have legal access to enter heaven because of Jesus, and we can only enter through Jesus. In addition, while we live here, we have both the power and authority to act on his behalf.

There are mysteries the Bible speaks of that have been revealed by God. One of those is mentioned in 1 Corinthians 2:7-8,

> *"We speak God's wisdom in a mystery, the hidden wisdom which God predestined before the ages to our glory; the wisdom which none of the rulers of this age has understood; for if they had understood it they would not have crucified the Lord of glory;"*

Listen to this mystery I have already shared, revealed in Colossians 1:27 reads, "To whom God willed to make known what is the riches of the glory of this mystery among the Gentiles, which is **Christ in you**, the hope of glory." So instead of having one Jesus to deal with, the enemy of God has to deal with Jesus in each and every believer.

So, if we are to establish or detail the "foundation" for a biblical church, this is it. Jesus is the Christ, the Son of the living God. Jesus is the gate, and this confession provides legal access to the kingdom of heaven. We have the authority and power to operate.

Just to glance back for a moment, we would be remiss if we did not look at what Peter has to say regarding the stone. It is worth looking at the longer passage of 1 Peter 3:4:8,

> "And coming to Him as to a living stone which has been rejected by men but is choice and precious in the sight of God, you also, as living stones, are being built up as a spiritual house for a holy priesthood, to offer up spiritual sacrifices acceptable to God through Jesus Christ. For this is contained in Scripture: BEHOLD, I LAY IN ZION A CHOICE STONE, A PRECIOUS CORNER stone. AND HE WHO BELIEVES IN HIM WILL NOT BE DISAPPOINTED." This precious value, then, is for you who believe; but for those who disbelieve, "THE STONE WHICH THE BUILDERS REJECTED, THIS BECAME THE VERY CORNER stone," and, "A STONE OF STUMBLING AND A ROCK OF OFFENSE."

This is a remarkable and exciting passage to tie in with our previous discussion. In this passage, we see another word used for stone. It is the word Lithos (λίθος) This is a term that means stone but is often referred to as a precious stone. That is the connotation here as we read verse 4 where we are called living stones, found the choice and "precious in the sight of God." In verse 5 we are told that we are the living stones; we are being built up as a spiritual house, and not just a house but a temple. That is why we are told it is a spiritual house for a priesthood. Then quoting Isaiah 28:16, we see this word again "precious stone." In this case, the cornerstone. The one who believes in Him will not be disappointed. We can see this confirms the foundation that we have laid. When we get to verse 8, we see a term change back to petra, rock. This precious stone, the cornerstone (lithos) used as the very foundation stone, becomes a rock (petra) of offense. Jesus is both the foundation of the saved and the lost. On Jesus, everything rests. In the confession of Peter, everything rests. He is the foundation rock on which the church is built, and He is the rock of offense. So everything comes down to what a person will do with Jesus. Whom do they say that He is?

I want to share 1 Corinthians 3:15-16, "Do you not know that you are a temple of God and *that* the Spirit of God dwells in you? If any man destroys the temple of God, God will destroy him, for the temple of God is holy, and that is what you are." And in Ephesians 2:19-22 reads,

> *" So then you are no longer strangers and aliens, but you are fellow citizens with the saints, and are of God's household, having been built on the foundation of the apostles and prophets, Christ Jesus Himself being the corner stone, in whom the whole building, being fitted together, is growing into a holy temple in the Lord, in whom you also are being built together into a dwelling of God in the Spirit."*

In the same way, the Shekinah glory (the Hebrew name for the presence of God here on earth) dwelt in the temple of Jerusalem, a temple made by human hands. It was to foreshadow the temple of the indwelling of the spirit of God within the temple of the church built up by living stones. Every stone individually indwelt by the same spirit of God being fit together for his purpose.

His purpose is to reach as many as possible who are still under the enemy's authority and the judgment of sin. We are on the team of God and on a rescue mission. This is part of the role of the church. The ministry of the church and the gifts poured out on the body of Christ. The living stones are ultimately for the building up of the body of Christ to accomplish the purpose of the great commission. We are to go make Christ known. We are to help those in darkness see the light who has come into the world that they too might come to answer as Peter did and say, "You are the Christ, the son of the living God." Nothing, NOTHING, is more important than that. Everything else is directed toward that end.

Jesus loved people so much that he laid down his life for us all. Listen to this powerful passage we find in John 15:13-17,

> ""This is My commandment, that you love one another, just as I have loved you. *Greater love has no one than this, that one lay down his life for his friends.* "You are My friends if you do what I command you. "No longer do I call you slaves, for the slave does not know what his master is doing; but I have called you friends, for all things that I have heard from My Father I have made known to you. "You did not choose Me but I chose you, and appointed you that you would go and bear fruit, and that *your fruit would remain, so that whatever you ask of the Father in My name He may give to you.* "This I command you, that you love one another."

While we are still here in this kingdom of darkness, we are to live in such a way that we are making an intentional effort to reach those still trapped. Matthew 5:13-16 reads,

> *"You are the light of the world. A city set on a hill cannot be hidden; nor does* anyone *light a lamp and put it*

under a basket, but on the lampstand, and it gives light to all who are in the house. "Let your light shine before men in such a way that they may see your good works, and glorify your Father who is in heaven."

The church has not only been called out of the world, but we have also been set apart for a Godly purpose and this purpose is uniquely tied to the salvation of those still lost. We are part of God's plan for their salvation. As we consider the idea of what the church is today. I would ask that you find a church that actively understands this mission and a church that preaches sound doctrine. I want to make the main point here that the church is responsible for carrying out the mission of God. The church has been given power and authority to accomplish this mission. Unfortunately, many churches have turned from this focus to the focus of growing a large church. They assume that this is a substitute or in some way fulfilling the call of a faithful church, but it is not. We do not disciple people to a church, or to a pastor, we disciple them to the shepherd, to a savior, and that is Jesus the Christ.

It is natural to share this with others that truly understand who Jesus is, what He has done, and God's love for them. The goal, as previously mentioned, is to bring people to knowledge so that they can answer the question that Jesus asked the disciples, "Whom do you say that I am?" Jesus did not ask them this question when they first met. He taught them and walked with them first. When they were able to understand, he presented them with the question. Even still, the disciples came to believe at different moments. They wanted to believe, but they struggled with their preconceived ideas of who God was versus who He actually is. Thomas did not come to fully believe until he saw the scars on his hands and side. We read about this in John 20:24-29,

"But Thomas, one of the twelve, called Didymus, was not with them when Jesus came. So the other disciples

were saying to him, "We have seen the Lord!" But he said to them, "Unless I see in His hands the imprint of the nails, and put my finger into the place of the nails, and put my hand into His side, I will not believe." After eight days His disciples were again inside, and Thomas with them. Jesus came, the doors having been shut, and stood in their midst and said,

'Peace be with you." Then He said to Thomas, "Reach here with your finger, and see My hands; and reach here your hand and put it into My side; and do not be unbelieving, but believing." Thomas answered and said to Him, "My Lord and my God!" Jesus ⁎said to him, "Because you have seen Me, have you believed? Blessed are they who did not see, and yet believed."

Speculation and doubt are part of the natural process of coming to believe. It is hard to come out of the darkness when that is all you have known.

Like me, I am sure you have gotten up to use the restroom in the middle of the night and had to shield your eyes when turning on the bathroom light. The light was so bright it was an offense. We would have much preferred to slink back into the darkness, but once the eyes adjust though, it is a different experience. The darkness seems foreign, and those things that once seemed so clear when your eyes were adjusted to the dark become hard to recognize.

Come to light, allow your eyes to adjust if necessary. For some, they would rather turn on the light trusting that they will be able to see things as they truly are and, in doing so, find out how right they are.

I want you to know that God loves you. The evidence of this love is Jesus the Christ. He came for one reason, to save us from the consequence of our sin and bring reconciliation and friendship with God. The consequence of sin can be removed. The only thing required is repentance, that is, turn from sin and turn toward Jesus. Ask Him to forgive you and apply the payment He made for sin to your sin debt. Thank Him for dying on that cross for you and ask Him to fill you with the holy spirit that you might live for Him. Whom do you say that Jesus is? Is He the Christ the Son of the Living God?

Being found as a believer in the Lord Jesus, you are called out of the darkness. The enemy no longer has any authority over you. You have been equipped to carry out the mission of God jointly with other believers.

There is so much more I want to share. I don't want to overburden you. If you can understand the things I have written, we have made a great beginning. God has sovereign authority. We were sold into bondage because of sin. Jesus came to set us free. We are now under the authority of Jesus. We have been given both power and authority to accomplish the continuing mission of Jesus. Walk in that power and in that authority. Do not become subjected again to slavery resulting from sin. If you have found that you have sinned or are entangled by sin, repent and confess your sin to your loving God. In doing so you will be restored. Your prayer will no longer be hindered due to sin. It is for freedom Christ has set you free. John tells us in 8:31-32

> "So, Jesus was saying to those Jews who had believed Him, "If you continue in My word, *then* you are truly disciples of Mine; and you will know the truth, and the truth will make you free."

Things to Come

As we have seen, the Bible talks about things in the past. The Bible also talks about things that will happen in our future. Like the past, prophecy in our future will happen as written too. Therefore, we need to understand where we appear to be in the timeline of events.

I want to start with a Bible passage in the book of Jeremiah. Jeremiah 25:1 Starts by stating, "The word of the Lord came to Jeremiah concerning all of the people of Judah." Chapter twenty-five tells us about the evil in the land of Israel and how the Lord has tried to get them to turn back, but since they refused, judgment is to come upon them. In verse 11, it reads, "This whole land shall be a desolation and a horror, and these nations shall serve the king of Babylon for seventy years." (Jeremiah 25:11). During the time of Daniel, this prophecy was historically fulfilled. As with many prophecies, we see historical and spiritual fulfillment. Daniel was praying about the time of captivity for the nation of Israel. Daniel was praying about this before the Lord and seeking answers for Israel's as a nation. That is important to understand.

In Daniel 9:24, the angel Gabriel came to Daniel and revealed to him what was to come for the nation of Israel. What he was talking about now was beyond Daniel's answers. It was taking him farther into the future of his people.

Please know that what I am sharing with you here is brief. There is much that can be taught on this subject. I just want us to understand that God, in his authority, has a plan in place that is coming into fruition even as we view our global circumstances today. In Daniel 9:24-27, we read,

> "Seventy weeks have been decreed for your people and your holy city, to finish the transgression, to make an end of sin, to make atonement for iniquity, to bring in everlasting righteousness, to seal up vision and prophecy and to anoint the most holy *place*. "So you are to know and discern *that* from the issuing of a decree to restore and rebuild Jerusalem until Messiah the Prince *there will be* seven weeks and sixty-two weeks; it will be built again, with plaza and moat, even in times of distress. "Then after the sixty-two weeks the Messiah will be cut

off and have nothing, and the people of the prince who is to come will destroy the city and the sanctuary. And its end *will come* with a flood; even to the end [4]there will be war; desolations are determined. "And he will make a firm covenant with the many for one week, but in the middle of the week he will put a stop to sacrifice and grain offering; and on the wing of abominations *will come* one who makes desolate, even until a complete destruction, one that is decreed, is poured out on the one who makes desolate."

Remember again, Daniel was seeking knowledge of the future of Israel, so this prophecy is regarding Israel. This passage of scripture refers to a period of time that is seventy weeks, a week is seven days so then seventy times seven for a total of four hundred and ninety.

Okay, so not to dive too deep, but we need to understand the correlation of one day being equal to a year. In the case of prophecy, a day can be equivalent to 1 year. We can see this principle taught in passages such as Ezekiel 4:6, "When you have completed these, you shall lie down a second time, *but* on your right side and bear the iniquity of the house of Judah; I have assigned it to you for forty days, a day for each year." And in Numbers 14:34, "According to the number of days which you spied out the land, forty days, for every day you shall bear your [1]guilt a year, *even* forty years, and you will know My opposition." Therefore, what we have in the prophecy given to Daniel by Gabriel has evidenced the same and is a four-hundred-and-ninety-year period. In Daniel, we read that a period of seven weeks and sixty-two weeks will pass until the Messiah is cut off. Seven and sixty-two is a total of sixty-nine years, meaning that when the Messiah is cut off, there will be one week left to be fulfilled for that seventieth week for the nation of Israel.

Here is where it gets tricky. Many people want to take the clear sense and make it into something different, so they can celebrate their personal insight into prophecy. Is my interpretation correct? I believe it is. Without too deep of an explanation, I will share with you why. I will explain what I believe we are told.

It is easy in the natural reading of the passage to understand that the seventy-year period is broken up into segments. After the sixty-ninth week, the Messiah, Jesus, was put to death. The prophecy was put on hold for an indeterminate period of time. This is due to what we commonly call the church age today.

We talked earlier about the fact that on the seventh day, God the Father rested. Once again, Genesis 2:2 reads, "He rested on the seventh day from all His work which He had done." We talked about the fact that Jesus has sat down at the Father's right hand. We read this account in Hebrews 10:12, "but He, having offered one sacrifice for sins for all time, SAT DOWN AT THE RIGHT HAND OF GOD"

We talked about the idea that we are currently under the administration of the Holy Spirit, leading mankind to the knowledge of truth in Jesus. In John 16:7-8, "But I tell you the truth, it is to your advantage that I go away; for if I do not go away, the Helper will not come to you; but if I go, I will send Him to you. "And He, when He comes, will convict the world concerning sin and righteousness and judgment."

After the church age is complete, the primary operation of the leadership of Jesus will begin again. This will be the beginning of the seventieth week of Daniel's prophecy.

There are, once again, different interpretations, as with all things future. What I am sharing with you is what I believe is clearly taught.

We are told that a time is coming when the church will be removed from the earth. There is a fairly well-known term today called the rapture, or the rapture of the church. The idea of the rapture comes from 1 Thessalonians 4:17, "Then ªwe who are alive and remain will be **caught up** together with them in the clouds to meet the Lord in the air, and so we shall always be with the Lord." In the Greek, the word is "αρπαγησόμεθα" or "harpagespmetha" which conveys the idea of seized or forcibly taken. While the word rapture itself is not a

Greek word, we should understand that in Greek, the word used is in the Future passive, meaning it is yet to occur but not by us. We actually get the word rapture from the Latin translation. The Greek word "harpagespmetha" is translated "rapere" in the Latin. From this word, we derive the word rapture.

As with other areas we have discussed, there are different interpretations of when the rapture will occur. The final week of Daniel's prophecy is typically referred to as the tribulation period. Some believe the rapture will be at the beginning of the tribulation period, some believe it will be in the middle, and some believe it will be at the end. The different views each use the Bible to substantiate their claims. It is not my goal to solve this issue in this book here. That would be for another time. What I want us to understand is that the rapture will occur. I personally believe it will occur at the beginning of the tribulation period for various reasons. I want you to understand that the final week of Daniel's prophecy is for the nation of Israel, not the church. When the church is taken out of the world, the transition of administration reverts back to the Lord Jesus. The Holy Spirit is the restraining force against the wickedness of Satan. As the body of Christ, the church is in the world filled with the Holy Spirit. When the church is removed, the restrainer will also be removed. In 2 Thessalonians 2:6-8, we read,

> *"And you know what restrains him now, so that in his time he will be revealed.*
>
> *For the mystery of lawlessness is already at work; only he who now restrains will do so until he is taken out of the way. Then that lawless one will be revealed whom the Lord will slay with the breath of His mouth and bring to an end by the appearance of His coming."*

I believe that the last week of Daniel will begin at the rapture of the church. It is tempting to give you what I see happening on the global scale right now today. I want you to know we see biblical truth and prophecy being fulfilled right now on a global scale. This reveals to us how far along we are or how close we are to the Lord returning for those who are his. PLEASE read the full passage in 2 Thessalonians. There are many important truths to learn. For example, read the description of the beast in Revelation 13:1-18, and then search the internet for a picture of the statue that has been placed in front of the United Nations.

We also have to understand that the church will be taken out of the world when the rapture occurs. Right now, there is a battle fought between those of the darkness and the children of the kingdom of light. This may sound far-fetched and mystically out there, but it is not. At some point, I believe in the near future, and the church will be removed and taken out of the way. The final week of the Angel Gabriel's prophecy to Daniel will begin. When the church is removed, the restraining force to hold back the evil will be removed, and things are going to go from bad to worse very quickly. The deceptive part is that for the first three-and-a-half-year period it will seem like all is well, but then.

What is my point in telling you this? I want you to know that we are seeing governments move right now to become a combined global governing body. As I write this chapter, there is a meeting coming of the World Health Assembly in less than two weeks. They are the governing body of the World Health Organization. They are voting to cede individual governmental sovereignty to the World Health Assembly. This means that the WHA and WHO will have authority that circumvents the constitution of the United States. It is said that the Chinese Communist Party, CCP, is presently pulling the string of the W.H.O. Other countries signing on to this agreement are the E.U., the U.K., and Australia. We also understand that the Global Reset agenda is being pushed for globally, and World Economic Forum, WEF states it will be in place by 2030. This is less than a decade away at the time of this writing. I do not know if the outcome of the meeting will accomplish there goals at this time, but it does reveal the agenda.

Please understand what I have written in this book. Pray about it. Weigh it against the Bible. Understand the reality of the battle or spiritual warfare for the souls of those trapped in the darkness by the bondage of sin. Understand that we can be free from the grasp of the enemy and come under the authority of Jesus, the Savior. We become a joint heir with Jesus. Not of the world but of the Word. The promises of God are true. His authority and his power reveal that what is written will come to pass. There is no grey area. There is no fence to sit on. There is no middle of the road. There is truth. The truth can set you free. Trust in the provision of God, the sacrifice of Jesus as a payment for sin. Ask God to forgive you of your sins and to come into your life, fill you with His Spirit and give you wisdom and discernment to walk with Him and become part of His kingdom. A child of light!

May God bless you richly in Christ Jesus.

Bibliography

New American Standard Bible: 1995 Update (La Habra, CA: The Lockman Foundation, 1995),. All further references from the Bible

Avery, Nathaniel. The Complete Books of Enoch (Annotated): 1 Enoch: The Ethiopian Book of Enoch, 2 Enoch: The Book of the Secrets of Enoch, and 3 Enoch: The Hebrew Book of Enoch (Collectors Edition) (p. 21). Kindle Edition.

Barnabas. The Epistle of Barnabas . CrossReach Publications. Kindle Edition.

Stedman, Ray C. *Body Life: The Book That Inspired a Return to the Church's Real Meaning and Mission*, Revised Edition. (Grand Rapids, MI: Discovery House Publishers, 1995),70.

Jeanson, N. T. 2016. *On the Origin of Human Mitochondrial DNA Differences, New Generation Time Data Both Suggest a Unified Young-Earth Creation Model and Challenge the Evolutionary Out-of-Africa Model. Answers Research Journal.* 9: 123-130.

MacArthur, John. 1 Peter MacArthur New Testament Commentary (MacArthur New Testament Commentary Series) (p. 210). Chicago, IL. Moody Publishers. Kindle Edition.

Supplemental Table 4 (Predictions of mtDNA differences under the YEC and evolutionary models) of the Jeanson paper shows an average of seven differences using a generation time of 35 years

Kim, H. L. and S. C. Schuster. 2013. *Poor Man's 1000 Genome Project: Recent Human Population Expansion Confounds the Detection of Disease Alleles in 7,098 Complete Mitochondrial Genomes. Frontiers in Genetics.* 4: 1-13.

Lightning Source UK Ltd.
Milton Keynes UK
UKHW022041310123
416280UK00020B/234